BLESS ME: ULTIMA

NOTES

- *Introduction to the Novel*
  A Brief History of New Mexico
  Witchery in the Southwest
  The Structure of the Novel
- *List of Characters*
- *Chronology*
- *Genealogy*
- *Maps*
- *Character Analyses*
- *Review Questions and Essay Topics*
- *Related Research Projects*
- *Selected Bibliography*
  Anaya's Major Works
  Critical Essays and Works about Anaya

by
Rubén O. Martinez, Ph.D.
Department of Sociology
University of Colorado at Colorado Springs

WILEY

Wiley Publishing, Inc.

Editor
  Gary Carey, M.A., University of Colorado

Consulting Editor
  James L. Roberts, Ph.D., Department of
  English, University of Nebraska

Production
  Wiley Publishing, Inc. Composition Services

CliffsNotes™ *Bless Me, Ultima*

Published by:
Wiley Publishing, Inc.
909 Third Avenue
New York, NY 10022
www.wiley.com

CONTENTS

Centerspread: *Bless Me, Ultima* Genealogy

BLESS ME, ULTIMA

Notes

LIFE OF THE AUTHOR

Anaya's Early Years. Rudolfo Alfonso Anaya was born on October 30, 1937, to Rafaelita and Martin Anaya in Pastura, New Mexico, a small village located on the western edge of the Llano Estacado (the Staked Plains). He was the eighth of ten children (three of them from previous marriages by his parents). Rudolfo was born into a generation of Mexican-American families that experienced the culmination of the displacement of an agro-pastoral, self-subsistence economy by a wage-labor market economy. His father tended to withdraw from this process, while his mother, a devout Catholic, encouraged Rudolfo to explore, adapt, and achieve in the enveloping social world of the Anglo American. Early in his life, his family moved from Pastura to Santa Rosa, where he spent his years as a boy.

In 1952, Rudolfo's family moved to Albuquerque, New Mexico. Already a teenager, Rudolfo found the city exciting and adapted quickly. Barrio life in the Barelas section of the city swept him into the fold of the urban life of Chicano/as. In 1954, a swimming accident left Rudolfo temporarily paralyzed and gave him time and cause to consider many philosophical questions about life and human existence.

Advanced Education (1956–72). Rudolfo graduated from high school in 1956 and enrolled later that year at a local business school. Unfulfilled by the study of business, he enrolled at the University of New Mexico to study English. There, he discovered the importance of literature as a means for expressing ideas. During his student years, he was influenced not only by his teachers, but also by the counterculture of the beatniks, especially by their anti-establishment poetry. In 1963, he received his Bachelor of Arts degree in English and began to teach at an elementary school in La Jolla, a neighborhood in southern Albuquerque. Anaya enjoyed teaching and went on to teach at secondary school levels. His interest in literature remained strong, however, and he eventually returned to the University of New Mexico for further study. In 1968, he received a Master of Arts degree in literature, and he returned later and earned another Master of Arts degree, this one in guidance and counseling. Between 1971 and 1973, he served as the Director of Counseling at the University of Albuquerque.

Writing *Bless Me, Ultima.* Although *Bless Me, Ultima* (1972) was Anaya's first published novel and the one that gained him international acclaim as a writer, it was not his first novel. His previously written novels did not see print. During the mid-1960s, he wrote prodigiously, expressing his life and his experiences through poetry, short stories, and novels. For Anaya, writing became an expression of freedom. Seeing his people around him "in chains," he revolted against that world. Breaking those chains was important; his characters would not be enslaved. He realized that if he could write about his experiences and his family, using the town where he grew up as a setting, he could focus on these early years and create a sense of being liberated. While doing so, he would also come to know himself better and better understand the forces that shaped him as a person yearning to write and yearning to be free. Using his childhood as the subject matter for a novel, Anaya put together a world filled with ideas and activity. *Bless Me, Ultima*, then, is a work that examines the various forces that shape the life of Antonio, a young Mexican-American boy who is a main character in the novel.

Bless Me, Ultima was begun as a story about Antonio, but it was Ultima who made the story click. Through Ultima, Anaya explored the subconscious world, that world below the surface of experience that contains his culture's collective images, symbols, and dreams. In this subconscious world, Anaya examines the cultural forces that shaped the lives of *Nuevo Méjicanos* and *Nuevo Méjicanas* in the 1930s and 1940s. Through Ultima and the subconscious world, Anaya exposes the dark side of *brujería* and raises questions about good, evil, and truth.

Initially, Anaya circulated the manuscript among the east coast publishers, but none showed an interest in it. Turning to Chicano publishers, he submitted it to Octavio I. Romano-V. and Herminio

Ríos, editors of Quinto Sol Publications, who were immediately interested in publishing the novel.

The Professorial Years. In 1974, two years after *Bless Me, Ultima* was published, Anaya accepted an invitation to teach creative writing at his alma mater, the University of New Mexico. Although he did not have a doctoral degree, Anaya was promoted to full professor of English, and, between 1990 and 1993, he served as the University's Regents Professor. In 1993, he retired from teaching and from working directly within the university system in order to promote literary work by Chicano/as. In 1980, he read from his works at the White House. Over the years he has received many awards, including a Kellogg Fellowship and the prestigious University of New Mexico Regents Meritorious Service Medal in 1990. In retirement, he continues to promote Chicano/a literary scholarship and study and continues his own creative writing.

A BRIEF SYNOPSIS

Bless Me, Ultima is about the social-psychological maturation of a Mexican-American, or Chicano, boy living on the eastern plains of New Mexico during the 1940s. The novel begins with Ultima, a *curandera*, or folk healer, going to live with the Márez family during the summer that Antonio is six years old. Antonio is preoccupied with and anxious about attending school and having to be separated from his mother. Related to these concerns is his engrossment with knowing his destiny. This concern is exacerbated by his mother's desire that he become a priest to a community of farmers, where her family lives. At the same time, Antonio is concerned about realizing the wandering desire that stems from his paternal lineage.

Antonio is nearly at the point of starting religious study for his first holy communion and is becoming concerned with good and evil in the world. Early in the novel, he witnesses the killing of Lupito, a war veteran, and fears that his father may be punished by God for being with the men who killed Lupito. Antonio is deeply concerned about the fate of Lupito's soul.

As the novel develops, Antonio's fears and concerns intensify and become woven together as he struggles to understand the events surrounding his life. He becomes preoccupied with questions about his destiny, life and death, and good and evil. Ultima conveys an indigenous viewpoint to him that provides guidance when he loses confidence in parental viewpoints and the teachings of the Church. Ultima tells him the stories and legends of his ancestors, and he comes to understand how the history of his people stirs his blood. Through her, Antonio learns the "old ways" and develops a new relationship with nature. This relationship opens him to the contemplation of the possibility of other gods.

Antonio learns there are powers in the world that differ from those honored by the Catholic faith. He helps Ultima perform a healing that saves the life of his Uncle Lucas, who had been bewitched by the Trementina sisters. Later, he witnesses another healing performed by Ultima and begins to understand the world differently; he learns to overcome his fears, especially his fear of change. In the end, Antonio understands himself and the world around him better, and he learns to accept life and the many challenges that it presents.

INTRODUCTION TO THE NOVEL

ABOUT THE NOVEL

Bless Me, Ultima is the first in a trilogy of novels which includes *Heart of Aztlan* and *Tortuga*. *Bless Me, Ultima* brings to literary life a search for personal identity in the context of the social changes experienced by Chicano/as in New Mexico during the 1940s, and is in some ways similar to Joseph Krumgold's *. . . and now Miguel*, which was published in the early 1950s, focusing on the life of a New Mexican teenage sheepherder. Anaya's story covers a two-year period at the close of World War II and centers on the experiences of a young, but serious boy who is attempting to make sense of the world around him and, at the same time, grappling with the opposing expectations of his parents. Anaya skillfully sets up a dialogue between Antonio and Ultima, the elderly healer who comes to live her remaining years with Antonio's family. It is to the wrinkled Ultima that Antonio turns to for advice as he tries to understand himself and the conflicts and contradictions around him.

The setting for the novel is the Pecos Valley in New Mexico. The valley is situated on the western edge of the Great Plains Province, which comprises the eastern third of the state. It is bounded on the west by the Southern Rockies and on the east by the bluffs of the Llano Estacado. The Llano is bounded on the east by the Canadian River and on the west by the Pecos River. The area is part of the Lower Sonoran zone of mesquite and black grama grass. Altitudes are below 4,500 feet, allowing for more grazing than do areas at higher elevations. The long, frost-free period, the fertile soil of the valley, and the high temperatures make the area an important agricultural zone. The flood plain of the valley is farmed and the plains of the Llano are grazed, with just enough water to permit both modes of production.

A BRIEF HISTORY OF NEW MEXICO

The earliest Indian and Spanish settlements in the Southwest are in the northwestern part of the upper Río Grande region. Ruins of early native civilizations can be found in Chaco Canyon, at Aztec, and at Mesa Verde, located in present-day Colorado. These were Pueblo Indians who lived in huge buildings (one ruin is estimated to have contained 800 rooms) and survived on an agrarian economy. In the upper Río Grande Valley, the Spanish explorers found some twenty pueblos when they arrived in the sixteenth century. They took refuge there from Comanche and Apache bands, whose nomadic lifestyles depended on hunting and stealing, and who were less friendly to foreigners than the sedentary Pueblos.

The earliest Europeans in the region wandered through it for years, after having been enslaved by natives near present-day Galveston, Texas. In 1527, Pánfilo de Narváez set out with an expedition of 300 men to conquer the provinces between the Río Grande and the cape of Florida. Early in 1528, the expedition explored the region near present-day Tampa Bay, where they heard stories about gold from the natives. Narváez, excited by the news of gold, separated his cavalry and infantry from their ships and spent the spring and summer months exploring the region. Near the end of summer, ill and tired from constant hostilities by natives, they built five barges near the mouth of the Apalachicola River and coasted westward in search of the Río Grande. They crossed present-day Mobile Bay and the Mississippi. Over time, the barges became separated and lost at sea. Early in November, Cabeza de Vaca and others, many sick and unconscious, were wrecked on an island near present-day Galveston, Texas. Approximately ninety of three hundred men on the five barges survived initially, but in the end, only four (Cabeza de Vaca, Estevánico, Dorantes, and Castillo) made it to Mexico City in July 1536.

Cabeza de Vaca, Castillo, Dorantes, and Estevánico, the black Moor from the west coast of Morocco, wandered through what is now Texas and the southern fringes of New Mexico between 1528 and 1536. In southern New Mexico, they crossed the Pecos River, some two hundred miles south of present-day Santa Rosa, New Mexico. Estevánico returned in 1539, with Fray Marcos de Niza for further exploration of the region. Tales of the "Seven Cities of Gold" excited the explorers, but they found only squalor and poverty in the small villages they visited.

In 1541, Francisco Vásquez Coronado led a full-scale expedition through the region after establishing his base in Pueblo Indian country. On his way eastward in search of Quivira, the fabled city with streets paved with gold, he visited the Pecos Pueblo, which is located west of the headwaters of the Pecos River. The expedition proceeded southeasterly into the plains and built a bridge over the Pecos River near present-day Puerto de Luna. Like Marcos de Niza before him, Coronado found only a few huts, none with gold.

Spanish settlement of the region began in earnest following the conquest of New Mexico by Don Juan de Oñate in 1598. Oñate and his men established a headquarters at San Juan, near the confluence of the Río Grande and the Río Chama. In 1599, the Spaniards subdued the native peoples at Acoma and established the first permanent colony of Europeans in the populous Pueblo Indian country. Over the next two hundred and twenty years, New Mexico became a region dotted with Spanish missions that were linked to the Pueblos. Professional soldier-citizens were given land grants for their services, and, through farming and stock-raising, they exploited Indian labor.

The province was divided into two administrative districts: the Río Arriba and the Río Abajo, which referred to the upper and lower portions of the Río Grande Valley and the adjacent districts. From Santa Fe, located in central New Mexico and at the center of the Pueblos, Spanish governors managed the affairs of the province until 1821, when Mexico gained its independence from Spain. Earlier, near the end of the seventeenth century, the Pueblos revolted and routed the Spaniards for approximately a decade. The Reconquest of 1692, by Governor Vargas, restored the regime of the Spaniards.

In August 1846, during the Mexican-American War, U.S. Colonel Stephen Watts Kearney took formal possession of New Mexico and granted citizenship and amnesty to anyone swearing allegiance to the United States. Over the next several decades, both Mexicans and Indians struggled to survive within the bowels of the new nation that conquered them.

Development of the region in the second half of the nineteenth century proceeded quickly under the influence of the Santa Fe Ring, a group of American bankers, lawyers, merchants, and politicians who promoted their interests in the region. Landgrabbing became one of the most lucrative activities among the members. In 1880, the railroad reached Albuquerque, and the following year, the Atlantic & Pacific Railroad and the Southern Pacific met at Deming, New Mexico. The region's population tripled over the next two decades as Americans migrated into the area in search of lands to mine, graze, and farm. Cattle barons on the eastern New Mexico plains provided beef on the hoof to Indians on reservations and soldiers at American military outposts.

The arid climate ensured that grazing would become prominent on the plains, with farming limited to river valleys until the introduction of well-drilling, which gave rise to new agricultural centers. The construction of dams in the late 1880s resulted in the impoundment of the Pecos River for irrigation purposes. It is during this time (1850–90), when the land was being developed and the hostilities between Americans, Mexicans, Navahos, and Apaches reached their apex, that the Puerto de Luna valley was settled.

The Agua Negra land grant was allotted to Antonio Sandoval on November 24, 1824, by the Republic of Mexico. On January 21, 1860, the land grant was confirmed by the Congress of the United States, with the acreage set at 17,631. In the spring of 1863, Mexican-American families moved to the banks of the Pecos River and established settlements on the Agua Negra land grant. The land was known to them and to their fathers, who hunted buffalo on the plains, and the settlers soon built homes and irrigation ditches and developed increasing acres of this new land. One of the later settlers was Don José Luna, from Los Lunas in Valencia County. His home became the stopping place for travelers, who called it *puerto de luna*, and the name later was extended to the settlement itself. In 1891, Guadalupe County was established out of a portion of San Miguel County, and Puerto de Luna became the county seat. That same year, the compulsory school act was passed, requiring youths to attend school. In 1903, the county's name was changed to Leonard Wood County, and Santa Rosa was made the county seat. In 1906, however, the name of the county was changed back to Guadalupe by the Legislative Assembly because the Anglo-sounding "Leonard Wood" was unpopular among the locals.

In 1912, New Mexico gained statehood after having been denied it twice before by the Congress of the United States. During World War II, New Mexican soldiers suffered the greatest number of casualties, especially during the War in the Pacific. In the early 1940s, Los Alamos, New Mexico, became the site for the Manhattan Project, which developed the atomic bomb. The first bomb was exploded on July 16, 1945, at Trinity Site, a location on Alamogordo Air Force Base.

Santa Rosa, the "City of Lakes," was settled in 1865 and is located 116 miles east of Albuquerque. It was named for a chapel built by Don Celso Baca, a prominent settler who dedicated it to St. Rose of Lima. Santa Rosa became the junction point of two important railroad systems, and railroad construction crews frequented the town regularly at the turn of the century. This activity declined as the network of highways begun in the 1920s was completed. Today, the city's greatest attractions are the numerous natural lakes in the vicinity, which are attended by interesting rock formations, trees, and shrubbery. The most picturesque is the "Blue Hole," a bell-shaped opening fed by a subterranean river. Locals believe that the lakes are fed by a common underground water source, and that they are connected by subterranean channels.

WITCHERY IN THE SOUTHWEST

Witchery in the Southwest has its roots in the Spanish and Native American cultures of the northern provinces of New Spain (which became the American Southwest). Spain's witch crazes differed from the witch crazes that occurred in Germany, France, England, Scotland, Switzerland, and other European countries during the fifteenth and sixteenth centuries. In those countries, millions of persons accused of witchery were put to death. The burning of Joan of Arc in France in 1431 probably best symbolizes these crazes. In Spain, however, there was only a spate of trials and burnings during the Inquisition. Indeed, the Spanish Inquisition's attitude toward "witches" looms as a beacon of enlightened reason when compared to the hysterias that prevailed in the other European nations.

Nevertheless, the Spanish reflected the views of the European Middle Ages and divided the universe into opposing forces of good and evil. They believed in monsters, giants, wild men, and dragons, and tended to associate witchery with women. For the explorers of the sixteenth century, the Devil had an earthly domicile, and sightings were reported in many areas of the New World. Like the Spaniards, the indigenous peoples of the Western Hemisphere held views of good and evil, but these forces were seen as part of life, found in every human and god. The Mayans believed in Ixchel, a death god equated by the Spaniards with the Devil, and the Aztecs held Tezcatlipoca as the lord of the night and the patron of the witches. In contrast to European views, witches among the Aztecs tended to be men. The Emperor Montezuma was himself a dabbler in witchery, and when he learned of the four-legged monsters with humans growing out of their backs (the Aztecs had never seen horses—nor men on horseback), he consulted his soothsayers.

Aztec witches were ordinarily held in high esteem because their black practices were believed to have been assigned by the gods. However, if they fell in disfavor or overplayed their role, they could be executed. To witches were attributed the powers to change themselves into animals, cause sickness and death, and fly through the air—sometimes in the form of a whirlwind. These superstitions were similar to those in Europe. Other commonalities included inducing illnesses. The methods differed, however, in that the Spanish used the evil eye (*mal ojo*) and jabbed dolls with pins while the Aztecs drew blood, introduced worms or pebbles into the body, or captured the soul. Other differences included the lack of organization and harmful qualities among those cultures in the New World. Spanish witchery was more organized and widely perceived as a general threat to social order. Witches were organized as bands of prostitutes, sexual deviants, and procurers. Old and New World forms of witchery melded together in New Spain and gave rise to a new body of supernatural lore.

Witchcraft (*brujería*), sorcery (*hechicería*), the evil eye (*mal ojo*), and other forms of occultism became part of the cultures of the Southwest. The use of potions, magic stones, dolls, the evil eye, black rituals, and other methods of witchery have been documented in the region for the past three hundred years. Spells of different sorts have been believed in by members of the populations in the region. A rain of stones has been part of this mythology. Medicine men and curers have been part of the folklore surrounding witchery and their perceived involvements in dark magic have varied with the movements against, and executions of, "witches" that have arisen from widespread fears of bewitchment. The connection between them is herbalism, which is linked to both medicine and witchcraft.

Witches, it was believed, could be born or inducted, with practitioners conducting schools for those who wished to learn the power of dark magic. Others could become witches by entering into pacts with the Devil. These were known as Satan's witches, and their compacts with the Devil were attended by ceremonial gatherings. Villages believed to be infested with witches were often associated with sightings of bright flickering lights, balls of fire, and ceremonies involving goats and snakes. People believed that witches facilitated their travel by taking on the legs and eyes of coyotes, cats, and other animals. They also roamed the skies as balls of fire. Owls were seen as allies of witches and, often, as omens of bad luck. Should a family hear the hooting of an owl over its rooftop, the members would interpret it as a sign that evil was about to visit the home.

Among the Chicano/as of the Upper Río Grande, Catholic Christianity provided a bulwark and protection against the evil work of witches. The cross was seen as the most effective safeguard against supernatural attack, and devout churchgoers believed themselves to be protected against enchantment. Men named "Juan" were believed to have special powers to catch witches, and when a spell was perceived, a "Juan" would be sent out to catch the witch who cast it. It was believed that black magic could be turned against its spellbinder, and if it was done, the fate of the victim was reversed to the person who dispensed it. In such an instance, the witch's evil boomeranged.

Brujería is part of the folklore of New Mexico and the Southwest. It has remained as part of the cosmological views that inform the practices of Chicano/as in the region. For instance, the practice of storytelling among families has sent many a chill down the backs of children, enchanting them with scary tales about the mysteries of the universe.

THE STRUCTURE OF THE NOVEL

The life of young Antonio Márez, like our own lives, is a multidimensional, booming, buzzing world—laced with constraints and opportunities, absolutes and relativisms, structures and freedoms, harmonies and conflicts, unities and divisions, consistencies and traditions, love and hate, good and evil. The primary structural feature of the novel is conflict—in the form of competing modes of understanding between farmers and cowboys, priests and healers, children and adults. War, too, is prominent in the novel. World War II is a distant ogre to whom U.S. citizens sacrifice their sons, and even if some of these sons returned, they were often poisoned with "war sickness." Indeed, there are tiny wars going on throughout the novel. One rages within Antonio, another among the students at school, and still another between the students and their teacher.

Antonio is caught between the competing lifestyles of his paternal and maternal families, and this conflict is embedded in the broader tension between Chicano/a and American cultures. His quest to understand takes him from a naive, innocent view of the world to one of increased knowledge and self-understanding. In the end, he learns that new outcomes can be formed from one's past, and that one should accept and gain strength from life rather than succumb to despair. Anaya seems to be saying that adversity and suffering can be productive and beautiful by making us stronger, wiser, and more sympathetic persons.

Anaya uses dream sequences to highlight the inner conflicts that push Antonio to understand the world around him. The dreams emphasize Antonio's acute intuitive sense, the conflictive understandings he has of the world around him, and his own deep fears. They are windows into Antonio's unconscious world as he matures and deepens his understanding. The dreams foreshadow many of the major events in Antonio's life.

Moments of profound revelation on the part of Antonio parallel the epiphanies felt by Stephen Dedalus in James Joyce's *Portrait of the Artist as a Young Man.* Indeed, Anaya himself writes about "epiphany in landscape," that profound sense of place that humans have with their environments—in particular, the relationship that Chicano/as have with the earth. The first epiphany occurs when Ultima opens Antonio's eyes to the beauty of the *llano* and the magic of the river valley. For the first time, Antonio feels the pulse of the earth and the unity between it and the various life forms, and he dissolves himself "into one strange, complete being."

The novel is written in a simple style that demonstrates the perceptive images of Anaya's understanding of the rural culture of Chicano/as in eastern New Mexico in the 1940s. It is bilingual in that it is interspersed with Spanish phrases and terms, but it lacks the fluid code-switching found in everyday life.

The autobiographical ethos of the novel has been recognized by many critical reviewers, and Anaya himself has been very explicit on this matter. The trilogy comprised of *Bless Me, Ultima, Heart of Aztlan,* and *Tortuga* has been acknowledged by Anaya as somewhat autobiographical in the sense that he uses the memories of his experiences as sources for his writings. His mother was from the Puerto de Luna valley, where Billy the Kid, *el Bilito,* attended Mexican dances and wrestled in the streets with his Mexican-American friends. Anaya's father was a *vaquero* who knew the hard work of the large ranchos on the plains. More affinities between the life of Antonio and that of Rudolfo can be traced, but the novel is not truly autobiographical, nor is it intended as such. Rather, it is a cultural novel that explores the ancestral heritage of Chicano/as and its relevance for their lives in the present. Much like Rodolfo Gonzales' epic poem, *Yo Soy Joaquin,* this novel frames an ethnic identity that resonates strongly with the Chicano/a readership in the United States. Other important Chicano/a literary works that address similar issues include Jose Antonio Villareal's *Pocho,* Sandra Cisneros' *House on Mango Street* (written from the perspective of a young girl), Richard Rodriguez' *Hunger of Memory,* and Mary Helen Ponce's *Hoyt Street: An Autobiography.*

LIST OF CHARACTERS

Antonio "Tony" Márez

The youngest of six children of Gabriel and María Márez. Six-year-old Antonio is a precocious boy who is intrigued by the events in his life and torn by several dilemmas that he faces during this period of his life. He is caught between the opposing destinies envisioned for him by his parents, and he struggles to find his own path. In the process, he serves as an "apprentice" to Ultima, adapts to going to school, makes his first holy communion, and witnesses several fatal events.

Ultima ("la Grande")

The elderly "folk healer" who comes to live with the Márez family. She has been a midwife to many women in the area and is sought for assistance by those who believe they have been cursed. She mentors Antonio during her final years.

María Luna y Márez

The mother of Antonio, spouse of Gabriel Márez, and close friend of Ultima. She is a devoutly religious woman with a strong conviction that Antonio should become a priest. She opposes the lifestyle of the cattlemen and seeks the stability and rhythms of farming.

Gabriel Márez

The father of Antonio and husband of María. Gabriel has given up the lifeways of the *vaquero*, but laments the loss. He believes the urge to wander in search of adventure is in his blood and is characteristic of his family. He dreams of going to California with his sons in pursuit of a new life.

Tenorio Trementina

The malevolent barkeeper who accuses Ultima of placing curses on his three daughters. He is driven by hatred and revenge. He kills Narciso and Ultima's owl.

Samuel

A schoolboy friend of Antonio who philosophizes with him and tells him the story about the golden carp. He is the brother of the Vitamin Kid and one of the magic people.

Cico

The mysterious friend of Antonio who takes him to the hidden pond where the golden carp lives. He tells Antonio the prophecy of the golden carp and the story of the mermaid at the Hidden Lakes. He is also one of the magic people. Like Ultima, he has clear, bright eyes.

León Márez

The first child of Gabriel and María Márez. He returns from WWII with the "sickness." He moves to Las Vegas, New Mexico, with his brother Eugene and later moves to Santa Fe with him and their brother Andrew.

Andrew "Andy" Márez

The second child of Gabriel and María Márez. He returns from the war and stays behind when the other brothers leave for Las Vegas. Later, when the brothers return, he leaves with them for Santa Fe. Antonio has a special relationship with him, which changes when Antonio witnesses Andrew's failure to perceive the urgency of a call for help by Narciso.

Eugene "Gene" Márez

The third child of Gabriel and María Márez. He also returns from the war and leaves with Léon to seek their fortune in nearby towns.

Deborah Márez

The fourth child of Gabriel and María Márez. Deborah has been in school for two years and now speaks only English.

Theresa Márez

The fifth child of Gabriel and María Márez. Theresa is learning English from Deborah.

Lupito

The World War II veteran who becomes deranged and shoots and kills the sheriff. He is shot and killed in the river near the Márez home.

Narciso

The friend of Gabriel Márez who tries to warn Ultima that Tenorio is out to do her harm. He is shot and killed by Tenorio as he is on his way to the Márez house to warn Ultima. He is one of the magic people.

Florence

The young member of the schoolboy "gang" who does not believe that God is just or that He even exists. He drowns in a lake while swimming with the other boys. He is a fair-skinned, blond boy with an angelic face.

Lucas Luna

The youngest sibling of María Márez. He is bewitched by the Trementina sisters and cured by Ultima.

Pedro Luna

A brother of María Márez and Lucas Luna. He is Antonio's favorite uncle. He mentors Antonio one summer and kills Tenorio when he tries to shoot Antonio.

Prudencio Luna

Antonio's maternal grandfather. He is the elderly patriarch of the Lunas.

The "Gang"

Horse, Lloyd, Bones, Red, Abel, Roque, Willie, the Vitamin Kid, and others. These are Antonio's friends and classmates.

CHRONOLOGY

The following chronology is based on the events in the novel with the frame of reference being the explosion of the first atomic bomb near Alamogordo, New Mexico, on July 16, 1945. The events in the novel have been temporally set in accordance with that date.

Spring 1945	May 1—the death of Hitler is announced by the head of the provisional German government.
	May 8—V-E Day, the formal end of the war in Europe.
Summer 1945	Ultima comes to live with the Márez family.
	Lupito is killed near the river.
	The first atomic bomb is tested on July 16, 1945, at Trinity, in the White Sands area near Alamogordo, New Mexico.
	July 26—Japan is given the Potsdam ultimatum of "unconditional surrender" by the Allies.
	August 6—The U.S. drops an atomic bomb on Hiroshima and, on August 9, another is dropped on Nagasaki.
	August 15—The Japanese surrender to the Allied forces.
	The Márez family goes to El Puerto de los Lunas to help with the harvest.
Fall 1945	Antonio starts school.
	Antonio's brothers return from the war.
Winter 1946	The Márez family is whole again.
	Spring 1946—Antonio's brothers get restless and plan to leave Guadalupe. León and Eugene leave for Las Vegas, New Mexico.
	Antonio and Andrew walk together into town in the mornings.
Summer 1946	The school term ends, and Antonio passes from the first to the third grade.
	Samuel tells Antonio about the legend of the golden carp.
	Antonio learns that Uncle Lucas has been bewitched and helps Ultima heal him.
	The struggle between Ultima and Tenorio is set in motion.
	Cico shows Antonio the golden carp.
	Ultima continues to teach Antonio about herbs and roots.
	One of Tenorio's daughters dies.
	Tenorio and his men threaten Ultima at the Márez home.

	The Márez family returns to El Puerto de los Lunas to help the Lunas with the harvest.
Fall 1946	Antonio returns to school.
	Narciso and Tenorio get into a fight at the Longhorn Saloon.
	Antonio and his classmates perform the Christmas play at school.
	Tenorio shoots and kills Narciso.
Winter 1947	Two of Antonio's brothers return from Las Vegas.
	Antonio returns to school after Christmas vacation.
	Tenorio tells Antonio that he will kill Ultima.
	Antonio begins catechism lessons.
Spring 1947	Florence questions the existence of God and pushes Antonio to consider other viewpoints.
	Antonio and his classmates make their first holy communion.
	Antonio goes to Agua Negra with Ultima and Gabriel to help a friend with bewitchment problems.
	Florence drowns at Blue Lake.
	School ends.
Summer 1947	Antonio goes to El Puerto to spend the summer with his Luna relatives.
	Antonio learns that another of Tenorio's daughters is dying.
	Tenorio kills Ultima's owl, and Ultima dies.

CRITICAL COMMENTARIES

Chapter 1   *Uno*

The novel opens with a mature Antonio narrating and recalling that period of his youth when Ultima, an old folk healer and midwife, came to live with his family. The night before Ultima arrives, Antonio dreams about the night of his birth, hearing again the loud, angry arguing between his mother's brothers and his father's relatives. His mother, María, is from a family of farmers living in El Puerto de los Lunas, and his father, Gabriel, is from a family of plains cattlemen in Las Pasturas. His mother's people revere the earth; they are rooted to it and depend on its crops. His father's family are restless and nomadic, inclined to be rootless and adventurous. Within Antonio flows the blood of two vastly different lifestyles. Which one will claim his soul? Antonio perceives that only Ultima, the woman who delivered him, knows the secret to his destiny.

After his father rides away to fetch Ultima, Antonio is saddened to think that soon he will begin school and will be separated from his mother, who is insisting that he and his sisters exhibit model behavior and great respect when Ultima arrives—especially Antonio, for he is destined, she says, to become a priest—a vocation that makes Antonio anxious and uncomfortable.

Upon Ultima's arrival, Antonio impulsively calls her by name—instead of "la Grande"—but Ultima insists that the boy means no disrespect, and she implies that she and Antonio share a special bond. Ultima brings her owl with her—a most unique owl, for it hoots only in a soft, songlike way, lulling the Márez family to sleep that night.

Commentary

The novel begins with a mature Antonio serving as a **raconteur**, or storyteller, recalling his youth. Anaya uses the **quasi-autobiographical** voice to capture the perceptual and intellectual limits of a young boy. The narrative voice is neither that of a retrospective, older Antonio nor that of the young, naive Antonio. It seems to be located somewhere between the two. The young Antonio is the **protagonist**, for whom the plot is lived reality. Childlike naiveté, curiosity, and spontaneity are used by Anaya to set the pace and direction of the narrative. Additionally, Anaya's diction and style contribute to the purpose of approximating the world of childlike perception and understanding.

Through the world of Antonio, Anaya skillfully describes the culture of the characters in the novel, their diversity in lifestyles, and the mores and norms that govern their lives. The religious emphasis captures the Catholic influence in their lives, as well as that of indigenous mysticism.

Symbolically, Gabriel Márez and the *vaquero* lifestyle represent the adventurous spirit of the Spaniards. Their wandering ways are marked by the free spirit that loves the wide expanse of land (or oceans). María Luna and her family represent the mystical rapport with the earth that is attributed to the Chicano/a indigenous *indio* heritage. At the same time, however, the culture is represented as an amalgam of European and Mexican influences, and their conflicts and contradictions are embodied in the lives of the characters. Gabriel, for instance, represents the lifestyle of the Spaniard, but has the viewpoint of the indigene. María, on the other hand, represents the lifestyle of the Pueblo, but has the religious viewpoint of the Spaniard (Catholicism).

The arrival of Ultima signals the start of a new period in the life of Antonio. This new period starts out in peace and harmony, with Antonio learning about the beauty of the environment. From Ultima he learns about the beauty of the plains, the power of the river, and the harmony between the plains, the river, and the sky.

Antonio's first **epiphany** occurs during his first summer with Ultima. She teaches him to feel the pulse of the earth and its beauty. Time stands still for him, and he feels a universal harmony in his existence. The fusion of past, present, and future is seen by some literary critics to have an affinity with Aztec cosmology, but Anaya has said that he did not study indigenous cosmologies as preparation for writing this novel. Perhaps, as claimed by literary followers of Jung, novelists sometimes unconsciously articulate symbols that represent archetypes from the collective unconscious. In this case, Anaya is consciously exploring the Chicano/a collective unconscious.

The chapter ends with Antonio dreaming of Ultima's owl, which he unconsciously identifies with la Virgen de Guadalupe, the saint of the land, whom he perceives as the embodiment of mercy and compassion. His association of the owl with the Virgen affirms his trust in Ultima's goodness. In local folklore, however, the owl is more often associated with "dark witches," signifying its evil nature. Anaya has deliberately broken with tradition and has offered an alternative meaning for a traditional symbol as a means of getting readers to contemplate other views.

(Here and in the following chapters, difficult words and phrases, as well as Spanish words and phrases, are explained.)

- **Ultima**   the last one, or the ultimate.

- **Está sola . . . ya no queda gente en el pueblito de Las Pasturas.**
  She is alone, and there are not many people left in the village of Las Pasturas.

- **vaquero** a cowboy.
- **big rancheros** ranchers with large haciendas.
- **tejanos** Texans.
- **llano** plains; in this case, the Staked Plains in eastern New Mexico.
- **Qué lástima.** What a pity.
- **llaneros** plainsmen; plainspeople.
- **crudo** hung over from drinking alcoholic beverages.
- **Ave María Purisima** a religious exclamation referring to the Blessed Virgin Mary; it is sometimes uttered when hoping to ward off evil spirits.
- **Es verdad.** It's true.
- **la Grande** the elder, used respectfully.
- **adobe** large bricks made of mud and straw.
- **el puerto de los Lunas** the refuge of the Luna family; a gateway; figuratively, it can mean a "gateway to the moon."
- **curandera** a folk healer.
- **chapas** chaps, as in cowboy chaps.
- **molino** a mill; in this case, a feed mill.
- **atole** cornmeal.
- **No está aquí.** He's not here.
- **Dónde está?** Where is he?
- **¡Madre de Dios . . . !** Mother of God . . . !; a religious exclamation.
- **Buenos días le de Dios.** God grant you good days; a greeting among New Mexican Chicano/as.
- **Pase . . . pase.** Come in . . . come in.
- **Nuestra casa es su casa.** Our home is your home.
- **cuentos** stories told as part of folklore.

Chapters 2 & 3 *Dos y Tres*

Ultima quickly settles into the family's workday routine, but takes sufficient time to teach Antonio about the herbs and roots she uses for her medicines; she also tells him that his spirit shares in the spirit of all things—including that of the river. Until now, Antonio has been afraid of the soul of the river.

One Saturday night, a drunken war veteran, Lupito, kills the sheriff, and Gabriel joins the sheriff's posse at the river. Antonio secretly follows his father and hides in some brush, where he sees the wild-eyed Lupito, holding a pistol and crouching close to the river bank. The deranged veteran screams a warning about Japanese soldiers when he realizes that the men have discovered him. The sheriff's brother says Lupito should be shot, that he is an animal; Antonio's father says that they should use reason, not force. Lupito rises, fires his pistol into the air to draw their fire—and is killed. Terrified, Antonio watches Lupito die, gasping and asking for Antonio's blessing.

At home, Ultima calms the frightened boy. Later, in a dream, he announces to his three older brothers, who are fighting far away in World War II, and who boast of their Márez blood, that it is necessary that he, seemingly only a Luna, like their mother, join them as they leave to build a castle on the other side of the River of the Carp; only he can "lift the waters of the muddy river in blessing" for their new home.

Suddenly, Antonio hears a lonely, chilling, unearthly howl, and his brothers cry out that it is the dreaded witch of the river—la llorona—seeking Antonio's soul. Then they cry that it is Lupito—wailing, as his soul washes downstream, still seeking Antonio's blessing. Antonio defies his brother's fears and, swinging a dark priestly robe across his shoulders, he commands the river to allow his brothers to cross and build anew.

Next morning before mass, Antonio's soul is filled with questions that seemingly have no answers. How can his father take communion when he has been an accessory to Lupito's death? Is he, Antonio, indeed destined to become a priest, a key figure in the peasant-farmer lifestyle of the Lunas? Why does his father value his Márez hopes and dreams more highly than his mother's Luna ideals? Why do some people say that Ultima is without sin, while others whisper that she is a witch? Confused about his mother's and father's antithetical concepts of worth, and confused about evil, the existence of God, and forgiveness, Antonio joins a group of rowdy boys who are gathered outside the church.

Commentary

The killing of Lupito is the major event in Antonio's life that sets in motion his preoccupation with sin and punishment. He is concerned about the salvation of Lupito's soul and the absolution of Gabriel and Narciso for their participation in the death of Lupito. Thrust into the role of priest by Lupito, Antonio becomes more and more obsessed with the trajectory of his destiny.

Religion is an important facet of Antonio's world. The church has been a powerful force in the lives of Chicano/as, and Anaya captures this dimension in the life of the Márez family. María, like many other Chicanas, maintains an altar at home. She and her family pray regularly before the altar, and their daily greetings and expressions are filled with religious references and sentiments. The centrality of the Church in the lives of the Márez family members and the surrounding communities is symbolized by its visible steeple and its tolling bells. Villagers' lives are organized and structured by the Church.

Antonio's dream that night reflects the importance of his brothers in his struggle for increased understanding. His brothers see him as a farmer-priest and call upon him to save them. Interestingly, it is the power of the river, primal and earthly, rather than the power of Catholicism which enables him to help them. This reflects his recent initiation, with Ultima as his mentor, into a spiritual relationship with nature.

Here, Anaya introduces la llorona as an important **motif** of ambivalence which, like the river, calls to Antonio and makes him fearful. Throughout the remainder of the novel, the wailing call of la llorona mixes with the owl's cry, the wind's mourning, and the church bell's tollings to both lure Antonio and to alert him to danger. La llorona is a mythic figure in Chicano/a and Mexican folklore. Many versions of the myth exist but all tend to be used as a device to socialize children, who are warned not to stray from or disobey their parents lest la llorona get them.

María and Gabriel hold conflicting views of human development. María thinks of growing up as a loss of innocence, whereas Gabriel views it as developing strength and self-worth. For María, Antonio is saved if he becomes a priest. For Gabriel, whose views have much affinity with those of Ultima, growing up is a fact of life, and it is not good that anyone should meddle in another's destiny.

In these early chapters, Anaya uses many Chicano/a riddles and sayings to depict the local culture. Anaya's intimate familiarity with and command of the local culture enhances his depiction of the family and infuses the novel with **costumbrismo**. The riddles and sayings merge with realistic characters to give them vivid, believable personalities. As the novel develops, the dialogue among the kids reflects their spontaneity, restlessness, bluntness, and sometimes vulgar behavior.

- **¡Amigo!**   Friend!

- **¡Andale, hombre, andale!**   Come on, man, come on!

- **farol**   a lantern.

- **la llorona**   the weeping woman; a mythical character alleged to have drowned her children, and not having been allowed into heaven, she is destined to search the river for their souls.

- **Lo mató, lo mató—.**   He killed him, he killed him—.

- **¿Pero qué dices, hombre?**   What are you saying, man?

- **sala**   a parlor; living room.

- **¡Un momento!**   One moment!

- **Ya vengo—.**   I'm coming.

- **Ya las campanas de la iglesia están doblando . . .**   Already the church bells are tolling . . .

- **Por la sangre de Lupito, todos debemos rogar . . .**   For the blood of Lupito, we all should beg . . .

- **Que Dios la saque de pena y la lleve a descansar . . .**   That God lift her punishment [or pain] and let her rest . . .

- **Hechicera, bruja**   Sorceress, witch.

- **Es una mujer con un diente, que llama a toda la gente.**   It's a woman with one tooth, who calls all the people; this is a riddle whose answer is: the church bell.

- **Arrímense vivos y difuntos/Aquí estamos todos juntos . . .**   Gather round living and deceased/Here we are all together . . .

- **chingada**   the screwed one; the reference is to Doña Marina, the Indian girl who served as mistress and translator to the conqueror of Mexíco, Hernán Cortes.

28

- **cabrón**   a pimp, pander, cuckold; someone who takes advantage of the weaknesses of others.

- **¡Hi-jo-lah!**   code for "hijo de la chingada," or son of the screwed one; an exclamation.

- **¡Ah la veca!**   code, or slang, referring to the penis.

Chapters 4 & 5   *Cuatro y Cinco*

One day in late August, while Antonio and Ultima are searching the hills for wild herbs and roots, he learns that even plants have spirits and that they must be told why they are being harvested; he is deeply impressed by Ultima's wisdom and begins to repeat her chants and imitate her walk. Sometime later, Ultima tries to explain to him why his mother's people and his father's people are so different; she likens the Lunas to the continually orbiting moon and the Márez to the restless, ever-changing ocean. Although Antonio lives on vast, empty plains, he is enchanted by both the moon and the ocean. Which will be his destiny? Later, during prayertime at home, he discerns a similar duality of contrasts between God, who is stern and not always forgiving, and the Virgin, who is loving and always forgiving. That night, he dreams that his mother is fervently praying to the Virgin, asking her to bring his brothers home. A voice assures her that the boys will return, and she, in turn, prays that Antonio, her fourth son, will become a priest. As he sees la Virgen praying over him, Antonio screams out in the darkness, and Ultima calms him.

Next morning, Antonio and his mother and sisters travel to El Puerto to help their Luna relatives with the harvest. Antonio is especially fond of his Uncle Pedro, who calls him "Tony." After dinner, María speaks of Antonio's becoming a priest and guiding the Luna family. When everyone has gone to bed, Antonio is comforted by the sound of Ultima's owl, gently hooting.

Commentary

In this chapter, Antonio, the **child-protagonist**, develops a spiritual relationship with the plants of the plains. Ultima becomes more fully his mentor and he learns the uses of the different plants and roots. Through her, he learns to feel at ease with the *presence* of the river and to work in harmony with the elements. From her, he learns about the ancient ways of his ancestors.

Antonio's thoughts about la Virgen de Guadalupe reveal his pre-occupation with punishment and forgiveness. For Antonio, God is a punishing, vengeful god, while la Virgen is forgiving. She represents purity, compassion, and mercy. Humans are born with sin which cannot be washed away except through one's holy communion with God. The dream reflects Antonio's emerging preoccupation with understanding whether or not he too is sinful and evil.

The dream, the third in the novel, reveals Antonio's concern about the souls of his brothers being doomed to eternal damnation. Antonio is concerned with the loss of innocence, the guilt that comes with sin, and his fear of death and the punishment of hell. His dream-death presents la Virgen in mourning over him, implying that she is requesting God to show mercy and forgive Antonio for his sins.

The trip to El Puerto reveals Antonio's fondness for Uncle Pedro and locates for the reader the sites of the brothel, the church, Tenorio's bar, and El Puerto. The spatial relationships among these sites set the geographic context for many of the events that occur as the novel develops. Anaya also provides graphic images of the communal activites that Antonio remembers from his previous visits.

The discussion at the Luna house affirms Antonio's association of his brothers with the loss of innocence. Uncle Juan expresses concern about Antonio's development and the need to prevent him from becoming "lost"—like his brothers. Antonio's peaceful slumber to the singing of the owl and under the watch of la Virgen associates the goodness of the owl with that of the Virgin. It also points to the sense of peace that he feels when he is with the Luna family.

- **la yerba del manso**   the plant of the lizard tail family; or, perhaps, a plant from Manzano.

- **arroyo**   a gully.

- **oshá**   a wild celery; a medicinal plant.

- **¡Mira! Qué suerte, tunas.**   Look! What luck, prickly pears.

- **álamos**   cottonwood trees, which bloom in late May and early June rather than in late summer.

- **manzanilla**   common chamomile.

- **mollera**   the membrane-covered separation between bone plates on the top of an infant's head.

- **chicos**   dried corn, usually cooked with beans.

- **muy sabrosos**   very tasty.

- **ristras**   a string of something, usually of chile.

- **cabritos, cabroncitos**   kids, small goats.

Chapter 6   *Seis*

On his first day of school, Antonio wakes with a sick feeling in his stomach; his parents are bickering about his future, and it is only after he hears Ultima enter the kitchen that he can rouse himself. Breakfast is clouded by Gabriel's insistence that Antonio is a Márez and María's fierce claim that he is a Luna, reminding her husband that long ago, when Ultima offered the "objects of life" to Antonio, the baby chose a pen and paper. Seemingly, Antonio is destined to be a scholar. Gabriel reluctantly agrees, nostalgically recalling happier times—before there was education, or fences, or railroads, or roads—when there was only the vast, windy plains of the llano.

Leaving for school and leaving his parents and Ultima behind is difficult; Antonio feels as though he will never see them again. Impulsively he dashes down the pebbled goat path toward the bridge and, half-way across, he is challenged to a race by a small, thin boy, called the Vitamin Kid. For a moment in the school yard, he feels lost in a sea of noisy children, but by noon, he has discovered with great pride that he can write his name. However, when Miss Maestas takes him to the front of the room and introduces him, speaking in English, the other children laugh. Antonio winces, feeling alone and alien. Later, the children laugh at the Mexican food that his mother prepared for his lunch. Behind the school building, Antonio finds a few other students who don't understand English, who feel like outcasts because they also are Mexican. In silence, they fight the loneliness that gnaws at their souls.

Commentary

Going to school is a major turning point in Antonio's life. He feels much anxiety about the impending separation from his mother, and he seems to have secretly hoped that magic would save him from the separation. At the moment when he is to leave home, Ultima blesses him and the girls, and he feels swept away by a whirlwind of ideas concerning evil, but reassures himself by remembering how to ward them off. He seems to perceive the llano as a demonic wasteland. As he leaves, he looks back upon his parents and knows intuitively that they will never be the same; something has changed in his life and it cannot be undone. Antonio perceives this next step in life in terms of good and evil. He associates good with the security of home and the warmth of his mother, and evil with the llano, the outside world.

As the tension between good and evil intensifies for Antonio, the river and the bridge increase in their symbolic importance. Initially, the river separates Antonio's house from the town and its evil people, but as he deepens his understanding, he realizes that the river both binds and divides. It is both a creative and a destructive force. In the end, the river will symbolize the irreversible passage of time and the human journey toward a final destination. Here, the bridge symbolizes Antonio's maturation, his transition from childhood to adulthood, and his shift from innocence to understanding. It is also the link between his Spanish-speaking world and that of the English-speaking townspeople.

The focus on family honor emphasizes the values of the culture. People are only as good as their family. The roles of the parents have become clearer, with the mother being the homemaker and the primary caretaker of the children. The conflict between the parents, while reflective of the conflict between men and women (that is, domination/subordination), is primarily caused by their characters (a *vaquero* and a farmer) rather than by their sex roles. Symbolically, masculine and feminine values are portrayed through the personalities. Ultima's character is emerging as an androgynous character, suggesting, perhaps, a solution to traditional gender conflict.

Antonio's walk to school gives the reader a sense of the route and of the people who will be part of that walk. The race across the bridge with the Vitamin Kid signifies a new period in Antonio's life. This new period is increasingly multidimensional as he develops new friends and new mentors. Antonio is preoccupied with his destiny as he leaves his mother's side to enter the outside world of school. Entry into the school is itself a tumultuous, chaotic event. Now cultural conflict between Mexican Americans and Anglo

Americans becomes a new reality for him, one that leaves him feeling different and lonely.

Anaya unobtrusively points to the acculturation and assimilation processes that now begin to have a greater impact on Antonio. We are alerted to the cultural tensions over language when Gabriel expresses disgust at the use of English by his daughters. At school, "Anthony" is what the teacher writes in her book, but "Tony" becomes his offical name in that strange outside world where lonely Chicano children haunt the rear of the school building. This loneliness is intertwined with his separation from his mother.

- **¡Ay Dios, otro día!**   Oh God, another day!

- **Llano Estacado**   the Staked Plains, located in eastern New Mexico and West Texas.

- **En el nombre del Padre, del Hijo, y el Espíritu Santo**   In the name of the Father, the Son, and the Holy Spirit.

- **¡Madre de Dios!**   Mother of God!

Chapters 7 & 8   *Siete y Ocho*

The news that the war is over brings great happiness to the Márez family; immediately María lights many candles, allows Ultima to burn incense, and insists that the whole family pray rosary after rosary together. The memory of the long prayer sessions segue into one of Antonio's dreams: he is at the river, where he hears the voices of his " lost brothers" saying that they are coming home from beyond the land of their father's dreams (California) , from the land of the golden carp (the Far East). They ask Antonio for his hand, his "saving hand"—and then, suddenly, with a crash, their "dark figures" tower above him. Antonio wakes in a fright and runs out into the cold night, where he sees his brothers cresting the hill, coming homeward.

Once more, the family is united. María is happy that Miss Maestas praises Antonio and that, once more, she can cook for the "lost sons," even though Gabriel talks continually of his dream to move the family to California. Winter comes soon, and happiness fades in the Márez household. Antonio's brothers sleep during the day and, at night, drink, play billiards, and spend many hours at Rosie's

Bless Me, Ultima
Genealogy and Pertinent Maps

The setting for this novel is the Santa Rosa area of New Mexico, a small town on the plains in the 1940s, where Anaya spent his early years before his family moved to Albuquerque. Note the triangle that can be formed by linking Santa Rosa, Pastura, and Puerto de Luna. Graphically, it is easy to imagine Antonio, growing up in Guadalupe (Santa Rosa), caught between two forces: the western pull of his father's people (Pastura) and the eastern pull of his mother's people (Puerto de Luna).

Note also the triangle that is formed by linking Santa Rosa with Anton Chico and Las Vegas, two towns that figure in the restless, nomadic lives of Antonio's brothers León and Eugene. Finally, note the location of Santa Fe, the capital city of New Mexico, where all three of Antonio's brothers hope to find their destinies, far from the small agricultural village where they grew up.

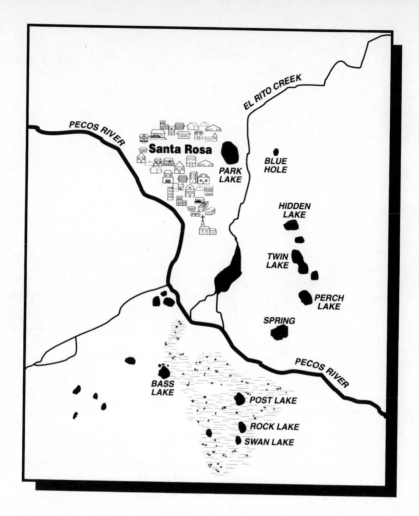

Water plays a strong, symbolic role in this novel. The root of *Márez* is "sea." Antonio's father tells him that he was baptized in the waters of the sea; his mother says that it was in the waters of the moon.

As you trace the loose necklace of lakes that hangs beneath Santa Rosa, recall the diagram that Cico draws in the sand for Antonio in Chapter II and the lakes' significance in the legend of the golden carp.

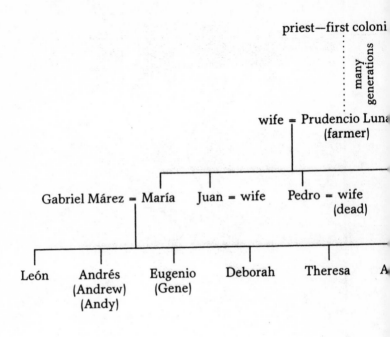

priest—first coloni

many generations

wife = Prudencio Luna
(farmer)

Gabriel Márez = María   Juan = wife   Pedro = wife
(dead)

León   Andrés   Eugenio   Deborah   Theresa   A
(Andrew)   (Gene)
(Andy)

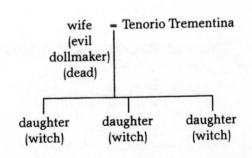

wife = Tenorio Trementina
(evil
dollmaker)
(dead)

daughter   daughter   daughter
(witch)   (witch)   (witch)

= married

Genealogy

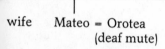

wife   Mateo = Orotea
               (deaf mute)

ıan

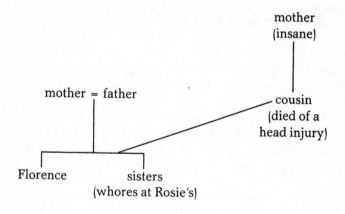

mother
(insane)

mother = father

cousin
(died of a
head injury)

Florence   sisters
        (whores at Rosie's)

whorehouse, incurring many debts. One of the brothers, León, has terrifying nightmares, and Ultima tends to him. Moody and restless, the brothers soon realize that they weren't meant to put down roots in this village. Their father's dream is unrealistic, while their mother's dream seems very realistic: Tony will become a priest, or a farmer, like the Lunas. They jostle and toss little Tony and teasingly ask him for his blessing before they strike out to seek their destinies elsewhere. Tony eagerly says that he will bless them—and they spank him and toss him on top of the chicken coop before they disappear down the road toward Rosie's, where they'll say goodbye to the girls. Instinctively, Antonio knows that they will become lost again. He longs to bless them—one more time.

Commentary

Antonio's brothers come home from the war and, for a time, make the family feel whole again. As the novel develops, María's religiosity becomes more and more evident. She prays regularly and orders the family to pray with her. Antonio's dream following one of these prayer sessions presents the giants of his infancy as lost and dying. The brothers thrust Antonio into the role of a priest by asking for his saving hand. Their dying reflects their lost social lives, and it seems to Antonio that they are being punished for wrongdoings. Their travel to the land of the golden carp foreshadows Antonio's introduction to its legend.

The return of the veteran sons revives Gabriel's dream to move the family to California. This possibility of moving intensifies Antonio's dilemmas about his destiny. The decision by the brothers to leave evokes a concern with obedience to parental authority and the possible repercussions for failing to do so. Antonio believes his brothers will be lost again, and he will be left to realize his mother's dreams, thereby absolving them of any guilt associated with failing to live up to parental expectations. Antonio assumes the role of priest and tries to bless them, but they laugh and take off to Rosie's whorehouse. Antonio is left with feelings of loss and vague associations between the breeding of cattle and his brother's relations with the girls at Rosie's. The spanking unconsciously reinforces the physical, sometimes violent, nature of sexuality. His understanding of what goes on at Rosie's house is still shallow, but he is beginning to make some connections.

- **¡Mis hijos!**   My sons!

- **Perdón.**   Forgive me; I'm sorry.

Chapters 9–11   *Nueve a Once*

In yet another of his dreams, Antonio's brothers appear. This time, they lead him to Rosie's house, joking and motioning for him to enter. Antonio cannot; he vows that he will preserve his innocence forever; he will become a priest. His brothers scowl and laugh at him: Tony is not only a Luna—he is a Márez; his wild Márez blood will someday burst forth—and even if he becomes a priest, a priest—because he is male—hungers to be fulfilled by a woman. The concept of innocence eludes the young boy; his mother has said that innocence lies in not knowing; the priest has said that innocence lies in understanding good and evil as God fills one's body at communion. In a flash of lightning, Ultima appears and tells Antonio that "in those hills [the lonely, wind-blown hills of the Las Pasturas llano] lies your innocence." Then she disappears, and Antonio longs even more fervently for answers to his aching questions.

He wakes and hears his brother Eugene shouting that he and his brothers must leave. They don't want to work on the highway with their father, and they don't want to follow their father's dream to go to California. They simply want to be out on their own. María cries and blames their father's wild Márez blood for their wandering, restless nature. Gabriel realizes that, without his sons, he will never realize his dream of moving to California.

In the morning, despite their parents' pleas, Eugene and León leave. Andrew stays behind because he knows how deeply his mother suffers the loss of her two sons. Soon he and Antonio set out—Andrew for a job at a grocery, Antonio to school. On the way, they talk of loss; Andrew says that he lost his innocence in the war; it is too late for him to become a priest. Antonio again wonders about his own innocence and when he will suffer its loss.

That spring, Antonio does so well in the first grade that he discovers, on the last day of school, that Miss Maestas has promoted him to the third grade. He is jubilant as he meets Samuel, who suggests they go fishing. Their poles set, Samuel tells Antonio that it is bad luck to fish for carp because long ago, when the world was young, the people in this region were given all they desired because they were faithful. They could eat everything—except the sacred carp. However, during a severe drought, the people were so hungry that they ate the carp. The gods were so angry they were going to kill the people until one god pleaded their case. The gods spared the people but turned them into carp. The god who pleaded their case was turned into a golden carp.

Antonio considers the possibility that his mother has been praying to the wrong god; perhaps she should pray to the golden carp. He asks Samuel where he can see the golden carp and is told that Cico will show him the fabulous carp. From that moment on, Antonio is obsessed with the concept of the holy, golden carp.

That summer, Antonio hears rumors that his Uncle Lucas is bewitched; he has been ill all winter and now it is summer, and he is still very ill, apparently because he watched some witches (the three Trementina sisters) dancing and performing "black rites." Ultima agrees to treat him, but warns Gabriel and María that they will be held responsible for perhaps unleashing an uncontrollable chain of events if she tampers with Lucas' fate. She says that Antonio will be her assistant, and Uncle Pedro stresses Antonio's strong Luna blood.

The horned day-moon that Ultima sees on their way to El Puerto seems a good omen; the Lunas have always cared for their crops and animals according to the cycles of the moon. After agreeing to a price for her services with Antonio's grandfather, Ultima and Antonio enter Tenorio's saloon, where she tells the owner that she has come to lift the curse that his daughters put on Lucas, and that they will suffer greatly for tampering with fate. She and Antonio leave and return to the Luna house; on the way, Tenorio dashes by them on horseback, racing home to warn his daughters.

After preparing an herbal remedy, Ultima feeds it to Lucas, who vomits it immediately. With confidence, Ultima tells Antonio that Lucas will be cured when he is well enough to eat the blue corn meal, which they are now eating. She will cure Lucas, she says, because good always triumphs over evil, even though the Church does not sanction what she does. Hearing Ultima's owl chase coyotes away from the house, Antonio falls into a deep stupor and assumes Lucas' sickness; he is seized by cramps, convulsions, and pain as Ultima attempts to heal Lucas by using Antonio's strong, healthy body as a surrogate in order to purge the dark, deep-rooted curse. Then she fashions three clay dolls, covers them with wax, and dresses them; she allows Lucas to breathe on them, while they seemingly writhe. Not long afterwards, she sticks pins in them, and Lucas vomits an enormous ball of hair, mixed with green bile. The witches worked their curse by using his hair.

Ultima bags the vile mixture and plans to burn it at the site where the dancing took place. Antonio senses that their work is done.

Later that summer, while fishing and wondering why Ultima could save Lucas' life and why the priest couldn't, Antonio is hailed by Cico, who offers to show him the golden carp—if he will take an oath never to kill a carp. Cico also wants Antonio to recognize the golden carp as a god, but Antonio can say only that he wants to do so. He must, ultimately, as a Catholic, recognize only God, the god of the Catholic Church. They stop briefly at Narciso's garden, eat carrots, then encounter some boys who taunt Antonio about Ultima's being a witch. Distressed, Antonio vomits bright yellow carrot juice and froth, and the boys are so repulsed that they flee.

At a large pond up the creek, Cico points to a dark, overhanging thicket; he says the carp will emerge from there. When it appears, Cico stands as if acknowledging a ruler; Antonio is so astonished at the carp's beauty that he feels as though he is dreaming. Both boys put their feet in the water as the gold carp watches them, then swims close to them. Cico then tells Antonio about the Hidden Lakes and about the mermaid who almost lured him to plunge into the lake. He explains about the immense power of the lakes, which is stronger than the presence of the river, and says that long ago, this land was beneath the sea, that it belonged to fish, and that someday, the golden carp will return to rule it once more. It will happen when the sins of the people weigh so heavily that the land collapses and the whole town is swallowed by the lakes. He draws a diagram, showing Antonio that their town is surrounded by lakes, and advises him to sin against no one. Ultima smiles when she hears the story and says that Antonio must find his own truths as he grows into manhood.

In his dream that night, he envisions a great lake and he sees the rotting carcasses of sinners on its shores. He hears the mermaid and sees the golden carp. Waiting for the appearance of the Virgen de

Guadalupe, he sees his mother, who says that those baptized in the holy water of the moon are saved. Gabriel, however, says that Antonio was baptized in the salt water of the sea, which links him to the pagan god, the golden carp. What blood runs through him—that of the moon? Or that of the sea? Ultima appears and explains that the waters of the moon gather into rivers and flow into the oceans, and then the waters of the oceans are drawn to the heavens by the sun to become waters of the moon again. Looking into Ultima's bright eyes, Antonio understands the old healer's wisdom.

Commentary

In the fifth dream, Antonio accepts the role of a priest as his destiny and resists being with sinful women. The brothers, however, remind him that he is a Márez and that some day he too will enjoy physical fulfillment by women; just as he chooses the priesthood as his destiny, he is told by his brothers that the Márez blood will ultimately prevail. Antonio's dream reveals an Oedipal guilt that surfaces when he sees the breasts of a young woman. His increasing understanding of sex between men and women that resulted from his last experience with his brothers is attended by fears of loss of innocence, a viewpoint attributed to his mother. Antonio's internal conflict over his destiny is intensifying. In this dream the three major sources of understanding in Antonio's world compete to influence him: María, the priest, and Ultima.

This dream foreshadows Andrew's decision to remain with the family but frames his stay in terms of Antonio's loss of innocence. He will leave when Antonio has become a man. Antonio is again torn between competing viewpoints. The brothers maintain that it is natural for men to be with women, and that becoming a man involves loss of innocence. In contrast, María sees Antonio losing his innocence by knowing about the sins of the flesh. Antonio wants to maintain his innocence and affirms that decision by refusing to enter the whorehouse. The priest, however, proclaims that Antonio is not innocent at all and must achieve innocence through holy communion with God.

Antonio's ever-growing concern with the contamination of his purity is plainly evident in his dream. He wants to know the path which will allow him to preserve his innocence. The priest emphasizes the rite of holy communion with God, but Antonio is unsure.

Overwhelmed by despair, Antonio is calmed by Ultima, who points to his roots in the plains as the location of his innocence.

Antonio's dreams are increasingly revealing the unconscious associations he makes as he grapples with the conflicts and tensions around him and their influences on his own fears and anxieties. He wants to preserve his innocence, yet unconsciously, considers the possibility of being evil himself. Indeed, part of his anxiety is caused by the increasing recognition that he himself is culpable and tainted with evil, as claimed by the Church.

The next morning Andrew and Antonio walk together into town. As they get to know each other better, Antonio has the opportunity to ask questions about his destiny. He hopes that their communion with one another will bring him understanding.

By skipping a grade in school, Antonio begins to fulfill his destiny as a person of learning. He also begins to demonstrate some independence when he decides to go fishing with Samuel. Both cognitive and emotional development combine to propel him to a level where initiation into the religion of the golden carp causes him to begin to raise doubts about Catholicism. These doubts begin just as Ultima is called upon to perform a healing. Antonio is drawn into a world of popular superstitions, magic, and the occult by virtue of the religious powers of his middle name, Juan. Ultima's healing of Lucas intensifies Antonio's skepticism about the power of the Catholic faith.

The conflict between good and evil becomes crystallized in the struggle between Ultima and Tenorio, both of whom embody Catholic and non-Christian views. Antonio's struggle to move toward independent critical thinking is intensified by the cosmic struggle that occurs through Ultima and Tenorio.

Understanding of this cosmic struggle is nurtured by the pre-Hispanic and prehistoric past contained in the legend of the golden carp, the knowledge of Ultima, and the content of the tales and superstitions of the people. This prehistoric past links Antonio to the physical landscape in powerful ways. The river's *presence*, for instance, is a manifestation of an "other" power. Ultima's life is close to nature, and Antonio is realizing that the forces of nature are very much a part of him and his world.

Witnessing the golden carp for the first time, Antonio revels in the epiphany of the moment. He feels a unity with nature that hitherto he had not experienced. However, at the very moment that he considers God and His reproach of pagans, the black bass arrives, signifying evil. Cico forces it to leave and harmony with nature is restored, with the boys soaking their feet in the water as the golden carp swims nearby.

As Antonio continues his initiation into the secrets of the past, he learns of the golden carp's apocalyptic prophecy, its concern with moral degeneracy, and the importance of remaining free of sin. Antonio is learning about a different moral order, one that competes with Christianity, and which sets him on a course toward understanding the relativity of thought. His dream pits the two moral orders against each other, and the tempest that arises from their conflict is calmed only by Ultima, who embodies both orders in a coherent unity.

---

* **bosque**   a cottonwood grove; a wooded area near water.

Chapters 12–14   *Doce a Catorce*

That summer is a season of knowledge for Antonio. He becomes more attached to Ultima than to his mother, and, from her, he learns the stories, legends, and history of his people. She cautions him never to touch the three dolls that she fashioned, and, from around her neck, she gives him her folk scapular, a thin pouch of cloth filled with sweet-smelling herbs, for his protection until he makes his first holy communion. Many afternoons are spent waiting for the golden carp to return, and during those months, Antonio listens to migrant workers talk of the social changes—the railroads and the barbed wire—that have ended the old way of life for his people.

One night, one of Ultima's friends, the town drunk Narciso, comes to warn her: one of Tenorio's evil daughters has died, and Tenorio blames Ultima. Outside, a shot is fired, men's voices are heard, and Tenorio demands that Ultima be given to them. Ultima comes to the door and, as Tenorio moves forward, her owl swoops down and gouges out one of his eyes.

Next morning, the family travels to El Puerto to help with the harvest; Gabriel accompanies them. They pass Rosie's whorehouse, and Antonio ponders the sins that will soon cause the town to sink into a lake of water. Like God, the golden carp punishes sinners; in contrast, the Virgin forgives sinners. Antonio thinks that the best god would be a woman.

One evening, after a day of harvesting, the adults talk about Tenorio's two remaining daughters building a coffin of cottonwood branches; witches, they say, cannot be buried in coffins made of pine, piñon, or cedar. They think that the sisters will probably perform a Black Mass, a ritual that Antonio dreams about. In his dream, he looks into a coffin and sees Ultima; simultaneously, he feels himself being picked up and comforted.

Next day, Antonio joins Ultima and other people on the street to watch the Trementinas as they approach—Tenorio on horseback, a black patch over an eye socket, and his two black-clad daughters in a horse-drawn wagon that carries a casket. At the church, the priest bars entry, and Tenorio turns his horse around, glances at Ultima, and vows revenge.

The harvest completed, Antonio returns to school, where he tells Samuel that he has seen the golden carp. Prophetically, Samuel warns him that schoolboys may soon taunt him into fighting about Ultima and her alleged witchcraft. Later, Tenorio and Narciso fight about Ultima in the town saloon, and Samuel tells Antonio that the conflict over whether or not Ultima is a witch will end only when blood is spilled.

The school Christmas pageant is chaotic, and, relieved that it is over, Antonio creeps slowly home through a fierce blizzard. In front of the saloon, he sees Tenorio and Narciso fighting in the thick, blinding snow and cursing one another. Eventually Tenorio leaves, threatening to kill Narciso and Ultima. Narciso braves the blizzard winds until he reaches Rosie's, where he calls Andrew to the door and warns him of Tenorio's threat to Ultima. Andrew, his arm around one of Rosie's girls, isn't unduly worried and goes back inside. Antonio follows Narciso silently as he leans forward into the icy wind on his way to warn Ultima. When they are on the goat path leading up to the family home, a shot rings out, men struggle, another shot is fired, and Tenorio flees. Antonio kneels beside the dying Narciso, who asks Antonio to hear his confession; afterward, Antonio makes the sign of the cross over him, then sobs uncontrollably.

Bursting into his mother's kitchen, he blurts out all that has happened, and that night, he has a nightmare: the girl at Rosie's pulls Andrew into the fires of hell. Antonio cries out to God, asking for

Andrew's forgiveness. A voice answers that Andrew is condemned to hell for eternity. If Andrew is forgiven, then Tenorio must be forgiven. The Virgin appears and says that she forgives all. God intervenes and says that vengeance belongs to Him—and not even the golden carp has His powers. As the flames of hell part, the blood of Narciso flows into a river, to be mixed with the blood of Lupito. A mob gathers, demanding Ultima's blood. Antonio sees his three brothers, whipped by three women, confessing to their sinful natures and asking for Antonio's blessing. The three Trementina sisters begin dancing around him, taking cuttings of his hair, which they mix with the blood of foul things. His body begins to wither and he dies without ever having taken holy communion. He is doomed to go to Purgatory. Meanwhile, the angry mob murders his father, mother, and sisters. They behead Ultima, drive a stake through her heart, and burn her body. Then they go to the river, catch the carp that swim there, cook them and eat them. The earth parts and the entire town sinks into the raging waters of the black void. The sun turns red. Farmers from El Puerto bury the ashes of Antonio's family, night falls, and the golden carp appears. It opens its mouth, swallows everything, and swims upward toward the stars. Its golden body becomes a new sun that shines upon a new earth.

Commentary

Antonio's preoccupations with Ultima's cure and the golden carp underscore his struggle to understand his world. As his enlightenment progresses, he realizes there are different views on how the world operates, and he struggles to decide which is the true one. He still believes that one's destiny is tied to one's blood, and his father continues to reinforce that view. Antonio finds refuge in the company of Ultima. He feels protected when he is with her, and he learns about the legends of his ancestors from her.

The family friends from Las Pasturas tell about the changes they have seen in life, and Antonio begins to realize that things never remain the same although he might not want them to change. He also learns of the grief that comes with change. Anaya is reminding the reader that broad sweeping changes in one's society bring turmoil and grief, and people must learn to adapt if they are to find happiness and harmony.

At another level, Antonio learns that nostalgia is a major element in the lives of people from Las Pasturas. Their approach to dealing with the predicaments of the present is to look to an idealized past. To a great extent, both Gabriel and María share nostalgic outlooks on their respective ancestries, and Antonio is beginning to understand this, but he does not necessarily commit himself to their strategy for coping with life's difficulties.

Tenorio's visit to the Márez home allows Anaya to express the traditional view of Mexican Americans regarding witchcraft, and it also allows him to use the scene outside the house to explore the mob-like tendencies among humans, especially when they are fearful of a person. These irrational tendencies continue to remain a mystery to us all.

The dialogue that occurs between Pedro and Antonio on their way to El Puerto makes clear Antonio's views on loyalty and social reciprocity. He believes strongly that his uncles should have warned Ultima about Tenorio because she helped one of their family members. He learns that others may put their own interests ahead of loyalty and norms of reciprocity.

The storytelling that goes on at the Luna household captures elements of the oral traditions of Mexican Americans and feeds Antonio's imagination. He dreams of the Black Mass and sees Ultima lying in a coffin, a scene foreshadowing Ultima's death and preparing Antonio for her loss, as well as for the acceptance of death, which comes for all.

The scene at the school, when the boys are closing in on Antonio, delves again into the group behavior of human beings and their willingness to scapegoat when they are fearful and ignorant of the causes of events around them. The discussion among the boys about witches and religion pushes Antonio further toward his realization of the multiplicity of views about existence. His fight with Ernie demonstrates his willingness to defend not only his own views, but also to defend those persons whom he loves.

The Christmas play exemplifies Anaya's ability to capture both the spontaneity and the rowdiness of young boys. It is a hilarious scene that brings some lightheartedness to an otherwise somber novel. The play stands in sharp contrast to the powerful storm that awaits outside.

The fight between Narciso and Tenorio sets in motion a series of events that dramatically affect Antonio. First, Narciso's call for help at Rosie's and, then, Andrew's appearance at the door of the whore-house shock Antonio. Not only does he realize that his brother has been sinning, but he feels a loss of his own innocence. Andrew's unwillingness to help Narciso drives a wedge between him and Antonio.

The murder of Narciso intensifies Antonio's inner struggle over justice and punishment. He is again forced to play the role of priest, and he gains some further familiarity with the role. As he matures, these experiences ground the decision he must make about his destiny.

The chapter ends with Antonio's eighth dream, which returns to the Day of Judgment. God's refusal to save Andrew from the fires of hell pushes Antonio to try to negotiate with Him. He promises to become a priest if Andrew is saved, but God will not hear the voice of someone who has golden idols. This part of the dream reveals Antonio's anguish over his initiation into the religion of the golden carp and foreshadows his realization that he too is a "sinner." Antonio continues to beg for the salvation of those persons whom he loves—his brothers and Narciso—but God will not save them. God tells Antonio that he wants both forgiveness for all and punishment for some—an impossibility. Antonio still believes in good and evil and the need to make punitive judgments against evil, and the dream sheds light on the limits of his ability to forgive. The Virgin, on the other hand, seems to realize that what appears to be evil is really ignorance and error, and this realization allows Her to forgive all.

In the next part of the dream, Antonio sees his own death and those of his family members. He is killed by the Trementina sisters and is doomed to go to Purgatory since he had not taken the Eucharist. This part emphasizes Antonio's anxiety regarding his own death and the importance of communion for salvation. In the destruction that follows, the wicked townspeople kill Ultima and her owl and feed upon the flesh of the carp; evil seems more powerful than good. In the end, no one from the town is left—only the farmers remain. The golden carp appears, however, and recreates everyone in a new form. And then he swallows everything, including good and evil, and becomes a new sun, shining down on a new earth.

The last part of the dream foreshadows Antonio's increased understanding of the world in which he finds himself. The golden carp is both vengeful and pure. It destroys the entire world so that it can be reborn. This suggests that destruction is a means of purification and that death must occur in order for rebirth to exist.

- **¿Qué pasa?** What's the matter?
- **¡Ay Dios!** Oh God!
- **¿Quién es?** Who is it?
- **¡La mujer que no ha pecado es bruja, le juro a Dios!** The woman who has not sinned is a witch, I swear to God!
- **¡Chinga tu madre!** Screw your mother!
- **jodido** one who is bad off in some way.
- **¡Mira!** Look!
- **¿Qué pasa aquí?** What's going on here?
- **¡Madre de Dios!** Mother of God!
- **abrazo** embrace, or hug.
- **the campo santo** holy burial grounds; a cemetery.
- **mitote** gossip; also a rambunctious dance.
- **¡Las putas!** The whores!
- **Ah la verga—** a reference to the penis.
- **¡Puto!** a sodomite; also, a promiscuous man.
- **¡Te voy a matar,cabrón!** I'm going to kill you, you jerk!
- **¡Hijo de tu chingada—!** Son of your screwed [mother]—!
- **¡Pinche—!** an expletive meaning damned, stingy, vile.
- **¡Por la madre de Dios!** For the mother of God!
- **huevos** balls, as in testes.
- **maldecido** a cursed person.
- **¡Ay que diablo!** Oh, what a devil!
- **Cabronas putas.** Pimped whores.
- **diablas putas—.** devilish whores—.
- **sangre** blood.
- **¡Dios mío!** My God!

Chapter 15 *Quince*

Sick with pneumonia, Antonio remains in bed for several days after his fever breaks. He learns that his father went to the sheriff and accused Tenorio of murdering Narciso; the coroner, however, declared that Narciso's death was the result of an accident or was self-inflicted. Narciso is buried, and the townspeople, who say he died drunk, quickly forget about him.

Andrew visits the bedridden Antonio but does not stay long. Afterwards, Antonio asks Ultima if he talked about Andrew while he was sick with fever. She says that he didn't reveal Andrew's secret, and he is glad that she understands.

After Antonio recovers, he sits with Ultima and listens to stories about the old days in Las Pasturas. She talks of Narciso's youth and how he turned to drinking after he lost his young wife to diphtheria. She tells Antonio of the strong social bonds that used to tie people together in lifelong friendships, bonds that helped them survive life on the desolate plains.

Antonio begins to recite prayers in preparation for his catechism class in the spring, and María asks him to read the prayers to her in English, even though she does not understand the language. She believes that Antonio needs to know both English and Spanish if he is to be successful as a priest.

One stormy morning before the end of Christmas vacation, León and Eugene are brought home by a police officer. They wrecked their car up near Anton Chico and had to burn it in order to stay warm. Afterwards, María prays to the Virgin, grateful for her sons' safety.

Next day, León, Eugene, and Andrew go into town to play billiards, and Gabriel drinks during most of the afternoon, happy to have his boys home again, but knowing they will leave in the spring, when he yearns most to go to the West Coast. Next morning, tending to the windmill, he realizes that the days when he and his sons could work together with pleasure are gone, and the next day, León, Eugene, and Andrew leave for Santa Fe. They didn't even wait until spring.

Commentary

Narciso's death goes unpunished by the townspeople, and Antonio becomes aware that social perceptions often determine justice. Because Narciso was a drunkard, the townspeople didn't care much about his death. Antonio, on the other hand, saw him as a good man and as one of the magic people.

Antonio becomes estranged from Andrew as a result of Narciso's murder. He cannot help but wonder if Narciso might still be alive if Andrew had helped him. Unconsciously, Antonio is blaming his brother for Narciso's death and finding it difficult to forgive him. Moreover, for Antonio, Andrew's departure affirms his loss of innocence.

From Ultima, Antonio learns of human frailty and how Narciso took to drinking to cope with hardships in life. He realizes that hardships bring people together and that lifelong friendships emerge as a consequence. But Anaya is also speaking to us about the social solidarity that exists in rural communities and the sense of community that stems from it.

Reciting his prayers in English to his mother, Antonio is reminded of the struggle over language. He is becoming increasingly aware of his membership in an ethnic group and developing a sense of the cultural conflict that exists. At the same time, his mother provides him with an adaptive strategy that embraces both Spanish and English. The return and departure of Antonio's brothers signify a new period in the Márez family. Gabriel seems to accept that his dream to move his family westward will never be realized and that his sons now have lives independent from his own. Gabriel works alone, and his solitude poignantly signals the end of the work team that he and his sons once constituted. For Antonio, the tension between the opposing visions and aspirations of his parents are bound to lessen, as Gabriel has achieved a new level of understanding and will not continue to stand resolutely behind his dreams. The brothers continue their own quests in life. Unconsciously, Antonio is losing confidence in his parents' nostalgic perspectives and in his brothers as role models. He is growing in assurance, critical intelligence, and individuality.

- **posole**   hominy soup, made with chili, pork, and spicy seasonings.

- **bizcochito**   homemade cookies sprinkled with sugar and cinnamon.

- **empanaditas**   turnovers, usually of pumpkin, fruit, or meat.

• **el policía**   the police.

Chapter 16   *Dieciséis*

School begins and Antonio feels older than his classmates. His thoughts cluster around the opposing concepts of good and evil; particularly, why God allows evil to go unpunished. He begins to pray more regularly to the Virgin, convinced that his first communion will bring understanding and answers.

Sitting under the juniper tree where Narciso was killed, dreaming of meeting the Virgin, Antonio encounters Tenorio and immediately forms a cross with a thumb and forefinger. Tenorio curses him and threatens to kill Ultima. Antonio rushes to warn Ultima and she wants to know if Tenorio touched him. She says that Tenorio returned to the juniper tree because his conscience knew that he had committed a mortal sin and it was seeking absolution. She assures Antonio that she will not be ambushed like Narciso.

Commentary

The pressures from his family somewhat lightened, Antonio continues to brood; he cannot understand why a good man like Narciso lost his life trying to do good, and why an evil murderer like Tenorio goes free and unpunished. Antonio begins to lose faith in God and begins to pray to la Virgen de Guadalupe, hoping that she will provide a sign that will help him understand. Andrew's absence exacerbates this gloominess.

His encounter with Tenorio brings the struggle between good and evil back to the center of his life. He fears Tenorio, but finds some solace in Ultima's courage. Antonio is beholden to Ultima for taking care of him during his illness and fears that Tenorio will harm her. Tenorio is brooding over the deteriorating health of one of his two remaining daughters and growing more and more resentful of Ultima. Anaya is setting up the climax of the struggle between Tenorio and Ultima.

The spring tempests, with their winds and moody skies, set a backdrop that infuses the moodiness of the boy with apocalyptic sentiments. It seems as though it is a time when the world could possibly end. As Antonio grapples with morose philosophical questions, Tenorio, the embodiment of evil, threatens Ultima and brings

Antonio back to the world of lived experiences. He must now face the absolute horror of Tenorio's evil.

- **maldito**   wicked, cursed.

- **desgraciado**   despicable.

- **entremetido**   a meddler, or intruder.

Chapters 17–19   *Diecisiete a Diecinueve*

In March, unusual, eerie dust storms become prevalent and Antonio hears adults blaming the atomic testing taking place south of Pasturas. The seasons have been disturbed, the old ones say, because man has gained too much knowledge, and too much knowledge will destroy mankind. Antonio's father cautions him not to blame bombs; man himself is to blame—for misusing the land and drying up wells. Deeply immersed in his catechism lessons, Antonio yearns for solid answers, for ultimate knowledge, and for direct, one-on-one communication with God. He feels certain that once he has taken communion, he will hear God's voice, speaking to him, unraveling the multitude of mysteries that confound him.

Antonio is adrift in a sea of confusion. He fervently wants to believe in God, but his friend Florence sternly and logically denies the existence of Heaven, Hell, and God. To Antonio's argument that God is continually testing our faith in Him, Florence chides that because God knows everything—there is no need for "testing." Antonio is more confused than ever because he understands Florence's logic, and he himself deeply desires knowledge—the original sin of Adam and Eve. At the same time, he believes in the godlike goodness and promise of the golden carp. Later, he witnesses a priest singling out Florence for undeserved punishment. Standing in the aisle, sunlit, his arms outstretched in chastisement, Florence seems like an angel to Antonio. Despite the priest's terrifying grains-of-sand analogy of eternity, Antonio realizes that Florence does not fear eternity. If Florence does not fear eternity and everlasting punishment, Antonio fears for his friend's fate and tries to convince Florence to at least believe in the golden carp—if in nothing else.

At last, it is Easter Sunday; Antonio wears new shoes, as well as his first new suit. On the way to the church, he meets several of his rowdy friends who joke about the catechism questions and demand that Antonio be their "priest," dancing and singing around him and confessing to voyeuristic sexual thrills. Confused and sickened by the vivid sexual talk on this holy day, Antonio tries to protect Florence when the boy is jeered at by his catechism-wise classmates. He states that, as priest, he can forgive Florence for blasphemy. Angered by his favoritism, the boys turn on Antonio and jerk his shirt off in a symbol of defrockment; then one of them jumps on his stomach and pounds his chest. Afterwards, Florence points out how ridiculous it was for Antonio to succumb to the boys' demand that he be their "priest."

During Easter Mass, Antonio is keenly aware that when the priest raises the chalice high, it no longer contains wine. It has become blood—not only Christ's blood, but also the blood of Lupito and Narciso. At communion, he is anxious as he receives the wafer and holds the saliva-slick body of Christ in his mouth. He knows, however, that he must complete this act if God is to speak to him. He swallows the wafer—and waits to hear the voice of God. Suddenly, he feels a poke in the back; it is time to move on. Others are waiting. The mass is ending, and God has not spoken to Antonio about the consequences of the death of Lupito, the evil of the Trementina sisters, the murder of Narciso, the defiant views of Florence, or the mystery of the golden carp. He calls to the God that is within him, but there is no reply. He looks at the statue of the Virgin, and the choir begins to sing. Easter Mass is over.

Commentary

Antonio is elated that he will soon make his first holy communion. He expects that the event will provide him with understanding and the world will then make sense to him. Catechism lessons intensify his conviction that communion will provide answers to his questions.

The pressures of change on the people are dramatized through apocalyptic interpretations of the detonation of the atomic bomb. Folk responses to the bomb link knowledge and destruction, and portend humankind's demise.

Gabriel's view of the dust storms and the plains expresses a regard for nature and its ways. Antonio learns that humans are part of nature and must assume responsibility for their actions, especially those that degrade nature. Anaya is expressing here aspects of the land ethics of New Mexican Chicano/as. The elders' views on the bomb, seasonal disturbances, and knowledge reveal many superstitious beliefs that inform them how the world operates. Antonio struggles to make sense of the world around him and is confused by the competing modes of knowledge that surround him. He wants to know which is the true view of the world.

Antonio's discussion with Florence makes him aware of the rational limitations of Catholicism. He realizes that he may share in Original Sin by virtue of his desire for more knowledge. Antonio is moving closer to the realization that he too has his own dark side.

When the priest punishes Florence, Antonio realizes that life is not necessarily fair. The angelic Florence is truly an atheist and an existentialist, and Antonio worries about his friend's soul. Ironically, just before he is to make his first holy communion, Antonio commits to showing Florence the golden carp as a means of giving him some higher meaning in life.

Antonio's first communion with God leaves him unfulfilled, and his faith in the power of God continues to diminish. He begins to realize that there are no absolute answers to his questions.

The episode with the group of kids causes Antonio to suddenly realize that Florence truly believes that he has not sinned. Antonio incurs the wrath of the other kids because he tries to protect Florence, and, in the process, he learns that he cannot be their priest. This incident provides him with a deeper understanding of the role of a priest and moves him closer to a decision regarding his own destiny.

- **Padre nuestro que estás en los cielos—.** Our Father who art in heaven—.

- **bulto** a wood carving of a holy person; also, a ghost.

- **Voy a tirar tripas—.** I'm going to throw up—.

- **gabacha** a white woman.

Chapter 20 *Veinte*

Each Sunday thereafter, Antonio attends mass, hoping to hear God, but each Sunday, he leaves unsatisfied, and soon school is out and it is time for him to travel to El Puerto, where he will spend the summer learning about farming from his uncles. He wonders about his destiny and tells Miss Violet, his teacher, that a man's destiny is like a flower unfolding itself to the sun, the earth, and water.

Antonio perceives the plains and the hills to be filled with life, yet senses a dark shadow over all their lives. He is worried about tracks near the juniper tree, where Narciso was killed, and about the news that old Tenorio's second daughter is dying. He is also disturbed when the rancher Téllez asks for Ultima's help in purging his house of what seems to be evil spirits who break dishes, cause a coffee pot to jump around and spill coffee, and rain stones down from the sky onto the roof of the house. A priest blessed the house, but the blessing was ineffectual; it changed nothing. Now, only Ultima can intervene and banish the evil.

Ultima explains that three lingering ghostly Comanche souls from long ago were improperly buried and now have been manipulated by the witch-like Trementina sisters to torment the Téllez family. She says that she can help Téllez, but she reminds the rancher that he must accept the consequences of her interference with destiny.

Antonio accompanies his father and Ultima across the plains and listens to them speak of their plains heritage and the inherent values that come from living on the plains. It is a conversation that is filled with hope and beauty, startling contrasts to what he experiences inside the Téllez house, as he listens to the rain of melon-sized stones on the roof. Calmly, Ultima tells the men to build a platform, upon which she will place three bundles, symbolic of the three Comanche men who were improperly buried. After setting fire to the platform, as was the Comanche tradition, Antonio hears Ultima's owl hoot. Her work is done. Téllez tells her that supernatural things began happening to him after Tenorio denounced her and he defended her honor about a month ago, in a saloon in El Puerto.

That night, Antonio dreams of his brothers, calling to him from the depths of the river, asking for release from their sea-blood. Tony tells them that he has no power and then baits his hook with their livers. They cry out in such pain that he removes the livers and throws them deep into the muddy waters of the River of the Carp.

Commentary

Antonio continues to seek answers through holy communion but finds none. He knows he is searching for something, but doesn't know what he seeks. With conflict both around and inside him, he withdraws from his classmates and becomes more and more obsessed with his questions. Turning to his school teacher for advice, he begins to develop sources of support outside the family.

Antonio feels that everyone is older, and this insight is confirmed when the Vitamin Kid is more interested in walking with a girl than in racing Antonio across the bridge. Antonio knows something has ended and he is saddened by the change. Anaya is signaling that an important period has ended in Antonio's life and that a new one is beginning. Antonio must now come to grips with change, the only real constant in life.

He spends time with Ultima, but senses that Tenorio is nearby, and he becomes worried about her, especially when he hears that another Trementina daughter is dying. The healing at the Téllez ranch, the second healing in the novel, affirms his view that Ultima's power is good yet different from that of a priest. His faith in the power of the Church continues to erode, yet he deepens his understanding of himself.

Antonio acknowledges the influences that Gabriel, Ultima, and his mother have had on him. He has learned to love the beauty of the plains and the knowledge that he is part of the earth. More and more, he seems to be moving toward the recognition that the views of his parents are compatible rather than mutually exclusive. As he develops cognitively, he moves from dichotomous, polarized views of reality toward the recognition of the dialectical unity of opposites and the relativity of "truth."

In the ninth dream, Antonio is unable to release his brothers from their wanderings. Instead, he casts himself as a provider of pain by baiting his hook with their livers and thereby causing them enormous suffering. Only by removing their livers from his hook is he able to release them from their agony. This dream reveals Antonio's new perception of himself as someone capable of punishment. Moreover, it reveals that he is beginning to accept change and fragmentation. He is unconsciously beginning to accept the wanderings of his brothers and his own loss of innocence. His maturation is measured by his willingness to accept the permanence of change.

- **Agua Negra**   Black Water.

- **¡Gracías a Dios que venites!**   Thank God that you came!

- **Benditos sean los dulces nombres.**   Holy be the sweet names.

- **yerba de la vívora**   a snake, or a rattlesnake, weed.

- **comancheros**   Indian traders.

- **grillos**   crickets.

Chapter 21   *Veintiuno*

On his way to the creek with Cico, Antonio hopes to see the golden carp; at the same time, he is obsessed with communicating, one-on-one, with the Catholic God—despite the fact that He did not cure Uncle Lucas or save Lupito or Narciso. Cico believes in many gods; the god of the Catholic Church, he says, is a jealous god who cannot live in peace with the other gods.

Arriving at the creek, they witness the arrival of the golden carp. To Antonio, it seems to be the embodiment of beauty, the god of here and now. He tells Cico that they must tell Florence about the golden carp. Florence needs at least one god, one that can bring beauty into his life.

They arrive at Blue Lake and hear frantic shouting. Florence dived and did not surface. Antonio sends Abel for the lifeguard, and moments later, Florence's body rolls to the surface, his eyes clouded and staring. After the body is pulled from the water, Antonio kneels beside it, makes the sign of the cross, and prays an Act of Contrition. Instinctively, he knows that his actions are futile because Florence did not believe in God.

Above, two hawks circle high in the blue sky. Antonio notices that Cico is gone and suddenly becomes sick. He runs back to town and to the river, wades across to the thickets of the brush and cottonwoods on the other side, and spends the rest of the afternoon grieving for his friend.

Commentary

Antonio's unanswered questions draw him toward the golden carp. He remains convinced that God determines who goes to

comes through living; it involves having sympathy for others and recognizing our mutual interdependence as human beings. Problems and difficulties in life are overcome by the magical strength of the human heart. It is Ultima's understanding which is the source of her magic.

With the Lunas, Antonio finds peace within himself, and his nightmares cease. He feels the rhythms of the universe by working the fields in accordance with the cycles of the moon. Although he affirms himself as a Márez, he knows the Lunas are also part of his being. He is at peace with himself on this regard.

His encounter with Tenorio reveals Ultima's identity as the night-spirit. Running to warn her, Antonio overcomes his fear of darkness and escapes the death call of la llorona. He runs with resolution because now he runs to fight evil, unlike in the early part of the novel, when he ran away from the horror of darkness and the death of Lupito.

Ultima's death marks the birth of Antonio's manhood. His initiation into a deeper understanding has begun. He is no longer afraid of death and does not have to look to the gods of his dreams for direction because he knows to look within himself and to life for strength. Antonio is able to accept Ultima's death as part of the great cycle that is revealed to him in his dreams. The universe is ordered and there is a purpose to everything, but human understanding discovers this truth only through a lifetime of experience. In the end, it is being at peace with oneself, others, and nature that makes one at peace with the universe.

- **Te doy esta bendición en el nombre del Padre, del Hijo, y el Espíritu Santo** I bless you in the name of the Father, the Son, and the Holy Spirit.

- **acequia** an irrigation ditch.

- **tío** an uncle.

- **¡Adiós!** Goodbye!

- **¡Hijo de la bruja!** Son of the witch!

- **¡Espíritu de mi alma!** Spirit of my soul!

- **velorio** a wake to honor the dead.

CHARACTER ANALYSES

ANTONIO

Antonio is a serious boy whose search for understanding is precipitated by several events in his life. He is searching for models to follow as he embarks on a quest for his destiny. Although many clues to the answers to his questions are provided in his dreams and in his life, he has difficulties understanding the world around him. To a great extent, he is a passive spectator of events rather than a person of action. Due to his incapacity to understand the world around him, he serves as an instrument of fate and others' wishes. In the end, he discovers that the world is incredibly complex and life is immensely difficult, and that he must assume independence of thought and responsibility for his actions, but these truths come through understanding one's self and one's history.

ULTIMA

Ultima's character is the most complex, and although the **deuteragonist,** or the character second in importance, she can be seen as the heroine of the story. Ultima is a person of action, the one who performs the healings and provides guidance to others. She is the one who nurtures Antonio's spiritual awakening.

Ultima is a strong, confident woman who uses her knowledge and power to do good in the world. Her character combines elements of indigenous and European cultures (that is, paganism and Catholicism) into a coherent unity that provides an alternative to the Church and to the rational, scientific knowledge of the Anglo Americans. Ultima can be seen as the scapegoat of a cosmic struggle between good and evil.

Ultima is described in detail by Anaya. She is very old and wrinkled. She has a brown face, black hair, withered hands, and brown teeth. She has clear, brown, laughing eyes which sparkle like those of a child. She has the sweet fragrance of herbs about her, dresses in black, with a shawl about her shoulders. She keeps her possessions in a large blue tin trunk.

Ultima's owl is a good owl, in contrast with the usual alignment in the culture of the owl with the dark side of life. Unlike other owls, hers hoots softly.

Ultima is a practical and helpful person. She has been a mid-wife, she is a healer, and she helps María with daily chores around the house.

TENORIO

Tenorio is the embodiment of evil. He is a man of action who serves as the **antagonist** against Ultima and Antonio. Little is known about him except that the villagers believe that his wife was, and that his daughters are, black witches. It is suggested in the novel that he is a warlock, but this is not made entirely clear to the reader.

Tenorio is a determined man who carries out his threats. He is tenacious and holds on to his evil aims despite having to invest lots of time to realize them.

Tenorio has a thin, hunched body. His face is thin and drawn, with tufts of beard on it. His lips are thin, and his eyes are dark and narrow, with an evil glint emanating from them.

CRITICAL ESSAYS

GENERAL ASSESSMENT

Bless Me, Ultima is a splendidly written novel that is at once **tragic, pastoral,** and **apocalyptic.** The novel begins with Ultima's violation of the maxim not to interfere with the destiny of any person. Her death at the end of the novel can be seen as a **nemesis**, or punishment. These events occur in the context of a rural people whose cultural relationship to nature is being greatly impacted by Western development. The folk response to massive social change is apocalyptic in terms of perception, and the novel is apocalyptic in that it promotes biculturalism as a synthesis of the conflict between cultures. The novel has excellent symmetry, good pace and action, and can be seen as a Chicano **bildungsroman.**

Bless Me, Ultima is not only regarded as a major contribution to the growing body of Chicano/a literature that emerged during the Chicano/a Movement (1965–75), but also is held as one of the works that set the canon for Chicano/a literature. Today, the novel is regarded as part of the emerging genre of cultural novels that explore the development of self and ethnic identity in a world of racism and antagonistic ethnic relations. The writings of Anaya, especially *Bless Me, Ultima*, have generated the largest response of interpretation and criticism of any work by Chicano/a authors.

Bless Me, Ultima can be analyzed at many levels from many angles. It is a rich novel that weaves social change, religion, psychological and cognitive maturation, cultural conflict, ethnic identity formation, and many other themes together into a coherent and believable story about a young boy. At one level, *Bless Me, Ultima* can be read as a romance novel that laments the passing of a societal period that is seen in the present through myth. It can also be read at the cultural nationalist level as resolving the historical conflict between the villages and providing a counterposition to the racist ideology of the United States. Finally, it can be seen as a fragment of an expressive Chicano/Mexicano culture that promotes storytelling and uses apocalypse as an ideological construct. Literary critics have found *Bless Me, Ultima* a fertile text for analysis. The names, figures, and objects of Antonio's world have yielded rich analyses of their symbolisms. In sum, the novel is a richly textured narrative that weaves many themes and subthemes and allows for different interpretations.

Anaya's Use of Imagery. Anaya uses powerful images to evoke a multiplicity of responses from his readers. He draws readers into the story through prophetic dreams, idyllic scenes of harmony, episodes of spontaneous horseplay among children, scenes of mystical dynamism, and episodes of violence and death. Each of them is richly detailed and provides readers with a sense of closeness to the characters and to the forces of nature.

Oppositional Forces. Opposition is a technique widely used by Anaya in the novel to create **conflict** at many levels. Antonio's parents are opposed in their backgrounds and in their visions and aspirations; religions are opposed in their viewpoints and demands on the individual; cosmic forces are opposed in the forms of good and evil; and forms of nature are opposed in their dry and fertile manifestations. The novel contains **psychological, social, cultural,** and **physical conflict.** Indeed, conflict is pervasive in Antonio's life.

Tripartites. Anaya uses tripartites to structure the novel. Again and again, things occur in "threes." There are, for example, three cultures, three brothers, three Trementina sisters, three prophetic dreams, three revelations of Ultima's identity, three Comanche spirits, three interferences by Ultima in the destinies of others, and so on. While numerology is not a salient feature of the narrative, it is clear that numbers structure the plot.

The Question of Autobiography. *Bless Me, Ultima* can be categorized as a "quasi-autobiographical" novel in the sense that a mature, older "I" serves as narrator for the experiences of the younger "I." A mature Antonio is narrating his experiences as a young boy, but the experiences are conveyed through the childlike naiveté of a six- to eight-year-old boy.

At another level, like many other novelists, Anaya himself admits that he used his personal experiences and those of others in his childhood to construct the story. In another sense, then, the novel is quasi-biographical, but the reader is never privy to the distinction between the real and the fictional because Anaya presents it all as fictional. It really does not matter much which is real and which is non-real, since what is worthy of note is that Anaya, like other writers, takes his own life as a rich repository of experiences from which he draws upon to construct his stories.

REVIEW QUESTIONS AND ESSAY TOPICS

(1). Identify the three major turning points in Antonio's life. Why are they turning points, and how is he changed from those points forward?

(2). Cultural conflict is evident throughout most of the novel. Identify the different manifestations of cultural conflict and how they impinge on Antonio's life.

(3). In what sense is *Bless Me, Ultima* a romance novel?

(4). What is the function of la llorona in the novel?

(5). What are some of the features of the Chicano/a family that are presented in the novel?

68

(6). What is paganism? Who are non-pagans, and what are the boundaries between pagans and non-pagans? Is Ultima a pagan or a non-pagan?

(7). What culturally specific rituals can be found in the novel regarding the dead?

(8). What are the views of Ultima and Gabriel regarding the relationship between humans and nature? How does María view this relationship?

(9). Why is Antonio so concerned about the loss of his innocence? What does losing one's innocence mean in literature? In life?

(10). Which are Antonio's three prophetic dreams? What do they predict?

RELATED RESEARCH PROJECTS

(1). Examine the impact of a free market economy on the agro-pastoral lifestyle of New Mexicans between 1870 and 1940. What are the cultural adaptations that they made in order to survive within the United States?

(2). There is a rich literature on la llorona. Using that literature, describe the function of the myth within Chicano culture.

(3). Gender relations among Chicano/as are generally patriarchal. How does Ultima's character fit within such relations?

(4). Examine the history of land grants among Chicano/as. What are the land ethics and land use patterns among this population segment?

(5). Examine the socio-economic status of Chicano/as within the United States. What are the primary determinants of their social status?

SELECTED BIBLIOGRAPHY

ANAYA's MAJOR WORKS

novels

Bless Me, Ultima, Tonatiuh-Quinto Sol International, Inc., 1972; Time Warner, 1994.

Heart of Aztlan, Editorial Justa Publications, 1976.

Tortuga, Editorial Justa Publications, 1979.

The Silence of the Llano (short story collection), Tonatiuh-Quinto Sol Publications, 1982.

The Legend of La Llorona, Tonatiuh-Quinto Sol International, Inc., 1984.

Lord of the Dawn, the Legend of Quetzalcoatl, University of New Mexico Press, 1987.

Alburquerque, University of New Mexico Press, 1992.

Zia Summer (forthcoming).

Rio Grande Fall (forthcoming).

critical articles

"The Myth of Quetzalcoatl in a Contemporary Setting: Mythical Dimensions/Political Reality," *Western American Literature*, Vol.33, No. 3, 1988, 195–200.

"At a Crossroads: Hispanos Struggle to Retain Values in the Face of Changing Lifestyles," *New Mexico Magazine*, June 1987, 60–64.

"Rudolfo A. Anaya," *Contemporary Authors: Autobiography Series*, Vol. 4, No. 4, 1986, 15–28.

"The Courage of Expression," *Century*, Vol. 2, No. 5, 1986, 16–18.

"The Light Green Perspective: An Essay Concerning Multi-Cultural American Literature,"*MELUS*, Vol. 11, No. 1, 1984, 27–32.

"Still Invisible, Lord, Still Invisible," *AMAE, Journal of the Association of Mexican-American Educators*, 1982–83, 35–41.

"The Writer's Landscape: Epiphany in Landscape," *Latin American Literary Review,* Vol. 5, No. 10, 1977, 98–102.

"The Writer's Sense of Place: A Symposium and Commentaries," *South Dakota Review*, Vol. 13, No. 3, 1975, 66–67.

70

plays

Who Killed Don Jose? (first performed by La Compañía, Menaul High School Theatre, Albuquerque; collected in *New Mexico Plays*, edited by David Richard Jones, 1989, 197–231, University of New Mexico Press, Albuquerque, New Mexico).

Matachines (first public reading October 19–22, 1989, Tucson, Arizona).

The Farolitos of Christmas (a short story first performed as a play by La Compañía, December 1987).

The Season of the Llorona (first performed in 1979 in Albuquerque, New Mexico).

CRITICAL ESSAYS AND WORKS ABOUT ANAYA

CABEZA DE BACA, FABIOLA. *We Fed Them Cactus.* Albuquerque, New Mexico: University of New Mexico, 1954.

CALDERÓN, HÉCTOR. "*Bless Me, Ultima* A Chicano Romance of the Southwest," *Rudolfo A. Anaya: Focus on Criticism,* ed. César A. González-T. La Jolla, California: Lalo Press, 1990, 64–99.

CANDELARIA, CORDELIA. "Anaya, Rudolfo Alfonso (1937–)," *Chicano Literature: A Reference Guide,* eds. Julio A. Martínez and Francisco A. Lomelí. Westport, Connecticut: Greenwood Press, 1985, 34–50.

CHAVEZ, FRAY ANGELICO. "Southwestern Bookshelf," *New Mexico Magazine,* March–April, 1973, 46.

DASENBOCK, REED WAY. "Forms of Biculturalism in Southwestern Literature: The Work of Rudolfo Anaya and Leslie Marmom Silko," *Genre,* Vol.21, No.3, 1988, 307–20.

GISH, ROBERT F. "Curanderismo and Witchery in the Fiction of Rudolfo A. Anaya: The Novel as Magic," *New Mexico Humanities Review,* Vol.2, No. 2, 1979, 5–13.

GONZÁLEZ-T., CÉSAR A., ed. *Rudolfo A. Anaya: Focus on Criticism.* La Jolla, California: Lalo Press, 1990.

HERRERA-SOBEK, MARÍA. "Women as Metaphor in the Patriarchal Structure of *Heart of Aztlan*," *Rudolfo A. Anaya: Focus on Criticism,* ed. César A. González-T. La Jolla, California: Lalo Press, 1990, 165-81.

JOHNSON, DAVID and APODACA, DAVID. "Myth and the Winter: A Conversation with Rudolfo Anaya," *New America,* Spring 1979, 76-85.

KLEIN, DIANNE. "Coming of Age in Novels by Rudolfo Anaya and Sandra Cisneros," *English Journal,* Vol. 81, No. 5, 1992, 21-26.

KRUMGOLD, JOSEPH. *. . . and now Miguel.* New York: Thomas Y. Crowell Company, 1953.

LATTIN, VERNON E. "The Quest for Mythic Vision in Contemporary Native American and Chicano Fiction," *American Literature,* Vol. 50, No. 4, 1979, 625-40.

_____. "Chaos and Evil in Anaya's Trilogy," *Rudolfo A. Anaya: Focus on Criticism,* ed. César A. González-T. La Jolla, California: Lalo Press, 1980, 349-58.

MÁRQUEZ, ANTONIO. "The Achievement of Rudolfo A. Anaya," *The Magic of Words,* ed. Paul Vassallo. Albuquerque, New Mexico: University of New Mexico, 1982, 33-52.

MARTINEZ, RUBÉN. "Interview with Rudolfo Anaya,"*Writers' Forum,* Fall 1987, 14-27.

_____. "Rudolfo Anaya, Chicano in China," *Writers' Forum,* Fall 1987, 8-13.

NEWKIRK, GLEN A. "Anaya's Archetypal Women in *Bless Me, Ultima,*" *The South Dakota Review,* Vol. 31, No. 1, 1993, 142-50.

RAY, J. KAREN. "Archetypal Patterns in Rudolfo Anaya's *Bless Me, Ultima,*" *Rocky Mountain Review of Language and Literature,* Vol. 32, No. 3, 1978, 159.

SIMMONS, MARC. *Witchcraft in the Southwest: Spanish and Indian Supernaturalism on the Rio Grande.* Lincoln, Nebraska: University of Nebraska, 1980.

TESTA, DANIEL. "Extensive/Intensive Dimensionality in Anaya's *Bless Me, Ultima,*" *Latin American Literary Review,* Vol. 5, No. 10, 1977, 70-78.

TONN, HORST. "*Bless Me, Ultima*: A Fictional Response to Times of Transition," *Aztlán,* Vol. 18, No. 1, 1987, 59-68.

TREVIÑO, ALBERT D. "*Bless Me, Ultima*: A Critical Interpretation," *De Colores,* Vol. 3, No. 4, 1977, 30-33.

VALLEJOS, THOMAS. "Ritual Process and the Family in the Chicano Novel," *Melus,* Vol. 10, No. 4, 1983, 5-16.

VASSALLO, PAUL. *The Magic of Words: Rudolfo A. Anaya and His Writings.* Albuquerque, New Mexico: University of New Mexico, 1982.

WILSON, CARTER. "Magical Strength in the Human Heart—The Framing of Mortal Confusion in Rudolfo A. Anaya's *Bless Me, Ultima,*" *Ploughshares,* Vol. 4, No. 3, 1978, 190-97.

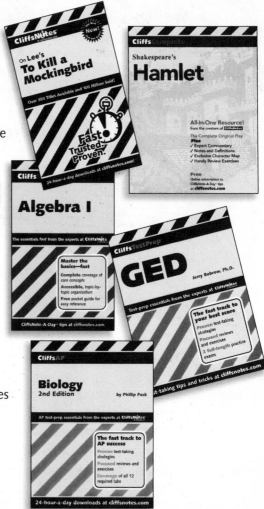

NOTES

NOTES